word processing

USING MICROSOFT® WORD 2000
OR MICROSOFT® OFFICE 2000

Rebecca Gilpin
Designed by Joe Pedley

Cover design by Russell Punter

Edited by Fiona Watt

Illustrated by Emma Dodd
Photographs by Howard Allman

Technical consultant: Cathy Wickens
With thanks to Nicola Butler, Ida McConnell and Lucy Owen
This is a product of Usborne Publishing Ltd., and is not sponsored by or produced in association with Microsoft Corporation.

Contents

About this book

Starting to use a computer can be a daunting and sometimes alarming experience, in which nothing seems to go right. This book eases you gently into the world of computers, using clear and familiar language, as it guides you through 30 useful and fun projects. Don't worry if you've never used a computer before, as the first few pages show you the basics of using one.

To find out how to do word processing using this book, make sure that you've got Microsoft® Word 2000. (If you're not sure what it is, read the next few pages to find out more.)

It's a good idea to work through the book from the beginning, as many of the later projects build on the earlier ones. You may be surprised to find that using a computer doesn't have to be hard work – it can be creative and great fun, too.

Useful features

STRANGE HAPPENINGS
If something unexpected happens, don't panic – take a look at the troubleshooting section on pages 60-61.

HANDY TIPS
If you want to find out more about Word and about its Help system, turn to page 58.

STRANGE WORDS
New computer words appear in bold lettering, **like this**. On page 59, they're explained, and translated into everyday language.

Tip

There are tip boxes scattered throughout the book. These give you handy hints.

What is word processing?

You may be wondering what word processing is, and why you might want to do it. Essentially, word processing is a way of creating things such as letters, letterheads, tables and newsletters, on a computer. This book shows you how to do word processing, using Microsoft® Word 2000, which you can get on its own or as part of Microsoft® Office 2000. On page 4, you can find out what Office is, and what other equipment you'll need.

Word is a way of organizing information on a computer. As its name suggests, it is mainly concerned with arranging words, but as well as helping you write letters, Word can also check your spelling, add pictures, and even help you to manage your accounts! Don't worry if this sounds complicated – this book will make using it simple and enjoyable.

The Spicy Food Fanatics Newsletter	12/12/00 _Spicy but nice..._

PIMENTO PRINCE AND PRINCESS CROWNED

On Saturday, the Pimento Prince and Princess were crowned in front of a huge crowd of almost 2,000 members of the Spicy Food Fanatics Society.

Josh and Hannah have both been

HOT STUFF IN THE KITCHEN – THE PEPPER TALK

We are very happy to announce that the guest speaker at our next Pepper Talk will be local chef Tom Tabasco. As many of you will know, Tom is well known for his strange and spicy recipes, and has been a chef

Accounts

Day	Going out	Food and bills	Transportation / Gas	Savings	Daily total
Monday	5.25	4.50	2.80	5.00	17.55
Tuesday	6.39	5.12	2.80	0.00	14.31
Wednesday	0.00	3.95	2.80	0.00	6.75
Thursday	3.50	4.95	2.80	0.00	11.25
Friday	10.00	3.45	2.80	0.00	16.25
Saturday	9.50	4.68	0.00	0.00	14.18
Sunday	0.00	2.25	0.00	0.00	2.25
Weekly total:					82.54

Happy Birthday

These pages were created using skills you will learn in this book.

The screen

As you work your way through the book, you may find that your screen doesn't look exactly the same as the ones that are pictured. Don't worry – this doesn't mean that there's something wrong with your computer – computers can be set up to show different colors and patterns on their screens.

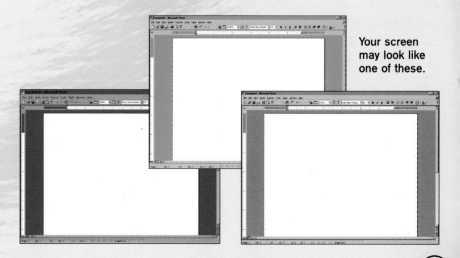

Your screen may look like one of these.

What do I need?

To use this book, you'll need a personal computer, or **PC**. There are other kinds of computers, but PCs are the ones most often used in homes and offices. A PC consists of several pieces of equipment. In computer jargon, this equipment is known as **hardware**. To make your computer work, you'll also need something called **software**. Software is the name for computer **programs**, which give your computer instructions.

Monitor

Hardware

This picture shows you what you'll need. All computers look slightly different, so don't worry if yours doesn't look exactly like this one.

This is the **system unit**. It contains the **hard disk drive**, which is where the computer stores information, and other parts that enable the computer to work.

The CD-ROM drive is used when you add software. Find out about it on page 62-63.

This is the printer. To print in color, you'll need a color printer.

Keyboard

This is a mouse. You'll find it easier to use if you put it on a mouse pad, but it will work on a table top.

Software

Software comes on a disc, called a **CD-ROM**, that looks like a music CD. You use the disc to load the software onto your computer. Once software is loaded onto your computer, the information stays there for you to use. To find out if you have the Microsoft® Word 2000 software already on your PC, turn to page 6. Microsoft® Word 2000 is available on its own or as part of Microsoft® Office 2000, which also contains several other programs. You'll also need a Microsoft® Windows® 95 or 98 operating system, which is a kind of software that enables other software to work. If you've bought Word, but don't know how to load it onto your computer, turn to pages 62-63.

Software comes on a disc like this one.

Plugging in

Make sure that the keyboard, monitor and mouse are properly connected to the system unit. Only push plugs into sockets of the same shape, and make sure that you don't damage the pins that are on some plugs. Don't plug the system unit and monitor into the main power supply until everything else has been connected.

The back of your computer may not look exactly like this.

Cable from the keyboard to the system unit.

Cable from the monitor to the main power supply.

Cable from the system unit to the main power supply.

Cable to the mouse.

Cable to the printer (see pages 18-19).

A cable links the system unit and the monitor.

You'll see extra sockets on the back of your computer. These can be used for extra parts, such as speakers.

If there are screws on a plug, make sure that you tighten them.

Color-coded plugs and sockets give you clues as to where to attach the cables.

Switching on

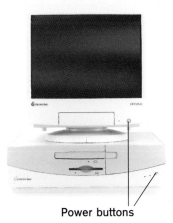

Power buttons

1. Press the power button on the system unit. If there is a button on the monitor, press that too. You'll hear noises as the computer gets ready.

2. Don't press any buttons – just wait for a few moments. The computer is ready to use when you see a Windows® screen like the one above.

Important

Although a computer has an on/off button, you shouldn't just switch it off when you've finished using it. There are various things you need to do before you switch it off, or you may find it difficult to switch on next time you use it.

See page 57 for instructions on how to switch the computer off.

Do I have Microsoft® Word 2000?

Now that you've switched on the computer, you need to see if you have Microsoft® Word 2000. To do this, you need to learn how to use the mouse.

Using a mouse

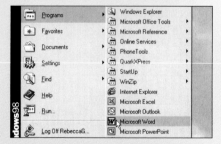

1. Place the mouse on the mouse pad or table. Rest your hand on the mouse. Your first finger should be on the left button, which you'll use a lot.

2. Move the mouse, until a white arrow appears on the screen. The arrow is called the **pointer**. The pointer moves as you roll the mouse around.

3. Press and quickly release the left mouse button. This is called **clicking**. Clicking is used when you want to tell the computer to do something.

Mouse fact

Sometimes people do funny things when they first use a mouse. They've been known to bang them on the screen, and to wave them in the air, like a television remote control.

Starting Microsoft® Word 2000

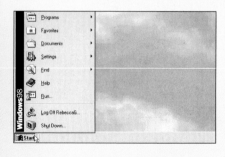
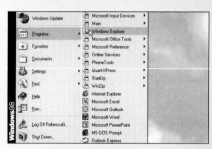

1. Move the pointer onto Start, which is usually in the bottom left-hand corner of the screen. Click the left mouse button. A list, called a **menu**, appears.

2. Move the pointer up, until it is over Programs, then click. A second menu appears. Move the mouse to the right. A bar appears over the second menu.

3. If Microsoft Word is on the menu, next to a W, move the pointer over it, and click the left mouse button. If it isn't there, turn to page 61.

The Microsoft® Word 2000 screen

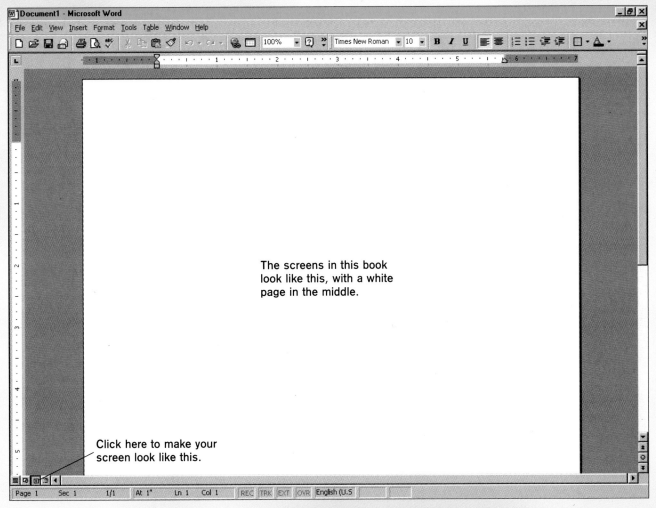

The screens in this book look like this, with a white page in the middle.

Click here to make your screen look like this.

4. The screen will change, until it looks something like this one. This is the Word screen. The white page is what computer people call a **document**.

5. On your screen, you may see an animated picture. This is called the Office Assistant, and it offers advice on how to use Microsoft® Word 2000.

6. You may see a message that says 'Start using Microsoft Word'. If so, move the pointer over the dot next to the message, and click.

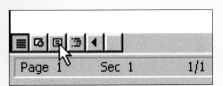

7. There are different types of Word screens. To make yours like the ones in this book, move the pointer over this square, at the bottom of the screen.

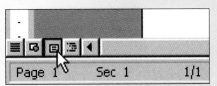

8. Wait for a moment. A little message saying 'Print Layout View' may appear. Click the left mouse button once. Your screen is now set up correctly.

Tip

The 'Office Assistant' offers advice, but it can be confusing. If you want to remove it, move the pointer over it, and press the right mouse button. A menu appears. Click on Hide.

Exploring the keyboard

You may be looking at your keyboard in amazement. There are letter keys in the middle, and they're surrounded by keys with signs and words on them.

Don't worry – as you work your way through the book, you'll find out how to use the keys that you need. You won't need to use some of the keys at all!

Pressing Caps Lock makes all letters you type into CAPITALS. Press it again to type normally.

The Tab key creates a space before you start to type. It's often used at the beginning of paragraphs.

The top row of keys are Function keys. You won't be using them in this book.

The Backspace key moves back one space, and removes whatever letter is there.

The Enter, or Return, key creates new lines.

Pressing the Delete key also removes letters, or whole words and sentences.

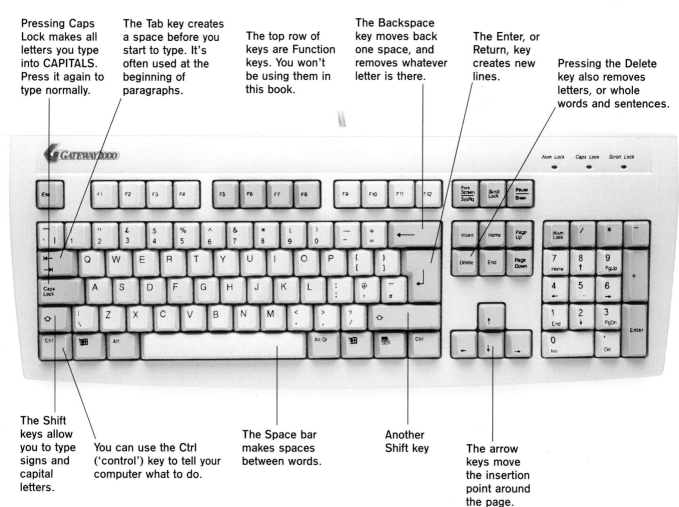

The Shift keys allow you to type signs and capital letters.

You can use the Ctrl ('control') key to tell your computer what to do.

The Space bar makes spaces between words.

Another Shift key

The arrow keys move the insertion point around the page.

Pressing a key

1. Look at the screen. On the white page, there's a small flashing line. This is called the **insertion point**. It shows you where your typing will appear.

2. Press any letter key, and watch what happens. As the letter appears on the screen, the insertion point moves on one space.

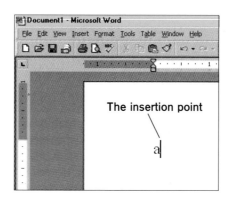

The insertion point

Tip

The lettering on the screens in this book has been made bigger, so that it's easier for you to read. As you work your way through the book, you'll find out how you can make your lettering bigger too.

Starting to type

Follow these steps to find out what happens when you use the keyboard. If you see colored lines that look like snakes, don't worry – just take a look at the tip box lower down the page.

1. Press any letter keys, one at a time. Don't worry about typing words. When the letters get to the end of a line, they start again on the next line.

2. To type capital letters, press the Caps Lock key on the keyboard once, and press letter keys. To return to small letters, press Caps Lock again.

3. To type just one capital letter, hold down one of the Shift keys, and press any letter key. A single capital letter appears on the screen.

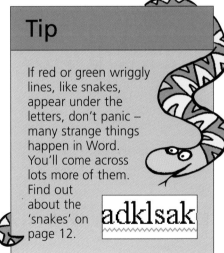

Tip

If red or green wriggly lines, like snakes, appear under the letters, don't panic – many strange things happen in Word. You'll come across lots more of them. Find out about the 'snakes' on page 12.

adklsak

4. To leave a gap under the letters you've typed, press Enter. Press it a few times, if you want to leave a bigger gap, then press some letters.

5. To make spaces between groups of letters, as you would if you were typing words, press the Space bar, then more letter keys. Try this a few times.

The Shift keys

As well as using the Shift keys to type capital letters, you can use them to type the signs that are on some of the keys. To type a sign, hold down a Shift key, and press any key with two signs on it. The sign at the top of the key appears on the screen.

If the key is pressed on its own, the lower sign appears on the screen. If Shift is held down as the key is pressed, the upper sign appears.

Using Microsoft® Word 2000

Microsoft® Word 2000 has a variety of features which will be new to you if you have used another version of Word, or a different word processing program. One main feature is that menus and **toolbars** change as you use your computer. Word 2000 remembers what you have used and reorganizes menus and **tools** to suit your needs. Tools can appear to go missing, but don't worry – they haven't disappeared altogether!

Menus

In this book, you'll be asked to click on options on menus. Menus are lists that appear when you click on the words at the top of the screen.

Usually it's easy to find the option you need, but sometimes options are hidden on longer menus. These steps show you how to see a long menu.

1. Move the pointer over the word Format, for example, at the top of the screen, and click the left mouse button. You'll see a menu.

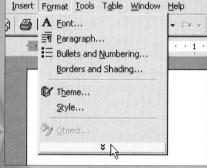

2. Now move the mouse so that the pointer moves down the menu and rests over the double arrow at the bottom. Click the mouse button again.

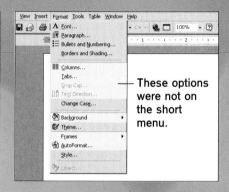

These options were not on the short menu.

3. A longer menu appears, with more options on it. New options appear on the light areas on the menu. These options weren't on the shorter menu.

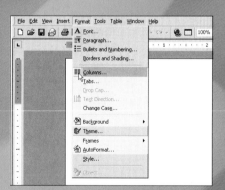

4. Now move the pointer over Columns, and click. A box appears on the screen, but you don't need to use it. Click on Cancel to make it disappear.

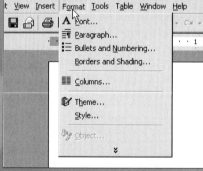

5. Click on Format again (see step 1). The word 'Columns' now appears on the short menu, because the computer knows that you've used it.

Menu tips

1. If you click on an option that is on a long menu, it will be on the short menu next time you look for it.

2. Don't be surprised if a short menu suddenly becomes a long one – this can happen if the pointer is resting on a menu.

3. To make a menu disappear, move the pointer over the white page, and click once.

Tools

Most of the tools you'll use are on the toolbar at the top of the screen, but you won't always be able to see all of them.

The tools you've used recently will be on the toolbar, but you'll often need to find tools that seem to have disappeared.

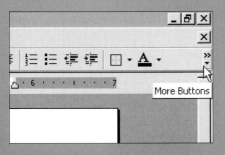

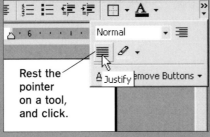

Rest the pointer on a tool, and click.

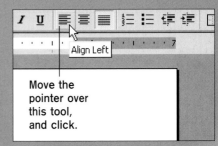

Move the pointer over this tool, and click.

1. Move the pointer over the double arrows that are next to the tools, near the top right-hand corner of the screen. Click the left mouse button.

2. More tools appear. Move the pointer over the Justify tool. A square appears around it, and a tiny message tells you which tool it is. Click on the tool.

3. The Justify tool is now on the toolbar. Click on the Align Left tool, to stop using the Justify tool. (You'll find out what this does on page 36.)

These are some of the tools that you'll be using in this book:

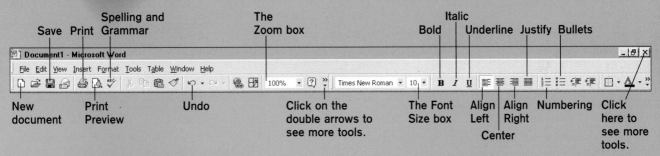

Save Print Spelling and Grammar The Zoom box Bold Italic Underline Justify Bullets

New document Print Preview Undo Click on the double arrows to see more tools. The Font Size box Align Left Align Right Center Numbering Click here to see more tools.

A new pointer

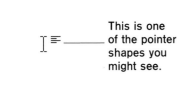

This is one of the pointer shapes you might see.

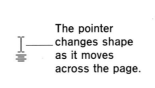

The pointer changes shape as it moves across the page.

1. Another new feature of Microsoft® Word 2000 is that the pointer changes shape when it's over the page. It has several short lines near it.

2. As the pointer moves, the lines change position. The lines show you how the pointer can help you arrange words on the page (see page 23).

Tip

Computer screens vary in size, and this can affect what you see on them. For example, if your screen is smaller than the one used in this book, you will see fewer tools on the toolbar. The tools are there, but there isn't enough room to see all of them. Follow the steps on this page, to see more tools.

1. An informal letter

This is the first project of many in this book – a Thank you letter. It's time to clear the screen, and type real words.

Clearing the screen

To clear the letters off the screen, hold down the Ctrl key, and press the A key. The letters appear in white, on a black background. Press the **Delete** key, to remove all the letters and clear the screen.

Removing the 'snakes'

The red and green 'snakes' that appeared on your screen are the computer's way of checking your spelling or grammar. They can be distracting, so remove them for now (see below). If you want to check your spelling when you've finished your letter, turn to pages 38-39.

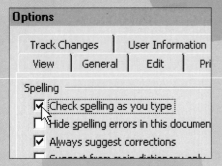

1. Move the pointer over the word Tools, at the top of the screen. A rectangle appears around the word. Click the left mouse button.

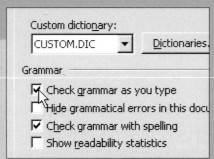

2. A menu appears. Move the mouse gently toward you, so that the pointer moves down the menu, until a dark bar is over Options.

3. Click the left mouse button. A large box appears. Move the pointer over the words Spelling and Grammar, near the top of the box, and click.

4. Move the pointer over the box next to Check spelling as you type. To remove the checkmark, click the left mouse button. The mark disappears.

5. Now move the pointer over the box next to Check grammar as you type, and click the left mouse button, so that the checkmark disappears.

6. Move the pointer over OK, and click the left mouse button. The Options box disappears. The 'snakes' won't bother you any more.

Writing the letter

Aspen House
|

1. Type the first line of your address. Find out how to type capital letters on page 9. Press the Backspace key if you make a mistake. Now press Enter.

**14 Beech Road
Woodville
WD1 2LL|**

2. Type the next line of your address, then press the Enter key again. Continue until you've typed your whole address at the top of the page.

WD1 2LL

Se|

3. Now press Enter twice, so that a gap is left under your address. This will make your letter look neater. Start typing the date, below your address.

Woodville
WD1 2LL

September
Sept|

4. As you type the name of the month, a tiny message may appear. This often happens in Word. Continue typing, and the message will disappear.

Dear Sam,

|

5. Press Enter a few times, then type 'Dear ...,' and press Enter twice. If the Office Assistant appears, click on Cancel, to make it disappear.

Dear Sam,

Thank|

6. Now you can start to type the letter. Make sure that you thank your friend for the present! If tiny messages appear, just continue typing.

7. If you want to start a new paragraph, press Enter twice, then continue typing. Add as many paragraphs as you want, then press Enter twice.

I hope you're well. We

Love,|

8. Type 'Love,' or 'From,' if you want to. You can sign the letter when it is printed on paper. Now turn to pages 14-15, to **save**, or store, your document.

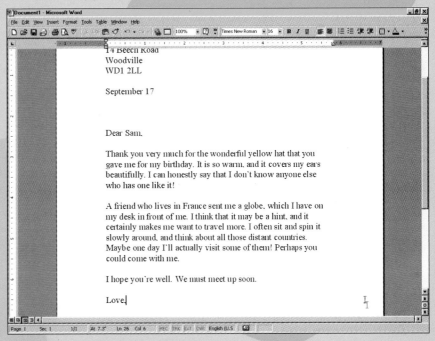

If you've written a long letter, you may not be able to see it all on the screen. On page 16, you can find out how to see different parts of your letter.

2. Saving what you've done

It's time to save your document, so that it is stored on your computer. When you save a document, you give it a name, and store it in a **folder**. This is where you may get confused. You might expect the computer to ask for a 'document' name, but it actually asks for a '**file**' name. It then stores the 'file' in a folder. Keeping a file in a folder may seem strange, so to avoid confusion, the word 'document' is used throughout this book.

Creating a folder and saving

Before you save your first document, you need to create a folder, in which you will save all your documents. A simple way to do this is to use the Save tool, on the toolbar at the top of the screen.

This is the name of a document, before you save it.

The Save As box is used to name and save what you've done.

My Documents is the name of the folder that Word saves your work in, unless you tell it otherwise.

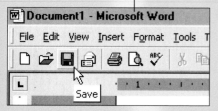

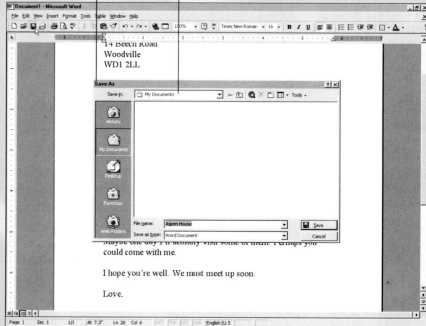

1. Move the pointer over this tool, near the top left-hand corner of the screen. A tiny message appears, which tells you that this is the Save tool.

2. Click the left mouse button once. The Save As box appears over your letter (see right). This is where you'll create a folder and save your work.

Click here to create a folder within My Documents.

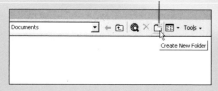

The name of the folder appears here.

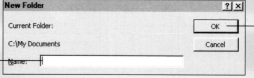

Click here when you've typed a name for your folder.

3. To create a folder, move the pointer over the Create New Folder tool, at the top of the Save As box. Click the left mouse button once.

4. A box appears, with New Folder in a white box. Use the keyboard to type a name for your folder. Type your name, or something you'll remember.

5. Move the pointer over OK, and click the left mouse button. The New Folder box vanishes, and you will see all of the Save As box again.

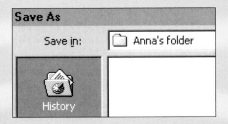

6. The name of your folder appears next to Save in, at the top of the Save As box. Now you can save your document in your new folder.

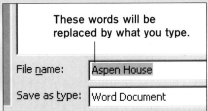

These words will be replaced by what you type.

7. Next to File name are the first words of your document. If there is a dark area over the words, type a name, then go to step 10. Otherwise, see step 8.

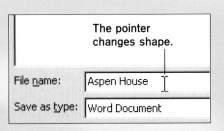

The pointer changes shape.

8. If there is no dark area over the words, move the pointer over the box beside File name. Move the pointer to the right of the words, as shown here.

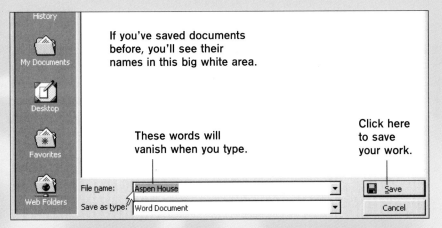

If you've saved documents before, you'll see their names in this big white area.

These words will vanish when you type.

Click here to save your work.

9. Hold down the mouse button, and move the pointer left, across the words. A dark area appears. Release the mouse button, then type a name.

10. Now move the pointer over Save, and click. The box disappears and the name that you typed appears in the top left-hand corner of the screen.

Tips

1. If people are sharing a computer, they can all create their own folders. This makes it easier to keep track of where things are. You can create as many folders in My Documents as you like, and save your work in your own folder.

2. When a dark area appears over a word, or group of words, you can type, and the existing words will disappear. Any words that you type will appear in their place.

More about saving

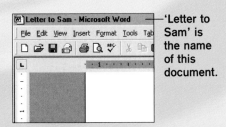

'Letter to Sam' is the name of this document.

If you've changed something you've saved, you can save it again, under the same name. Just hold down the Ctrl key, and press S. It is saved again.

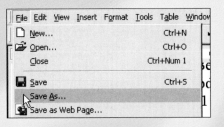

1. If you've made changes, and want to save the new version without losing the original one, click on File, at the top of the screen. Now click on Save As.

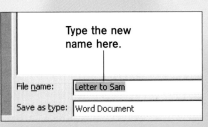

Type the new name here.

2. The Save As box appears. The name of the document is next to File name. Type a new name, then click on Save. Both versions are now saved.

3. Making corrections

You may find that you've made some mistakes in your letter, or you may just want to make some changes. On these pages, you'll find out how to add and remove words. Save any changes you make, as you go along (see 'Saving changes' on page 17).

Adding a word

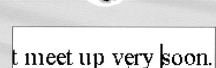

The insertion point

This word has been added to the letter.

On the keyboard there are four keys together, with arrows on them. The **arrow keys** can be used to move the insertion point around a document.

1. To move the insertion point up one line, press the up arrow key. To move the insertion point to the left, press the left arrow key, and so on.

2. Use the arrow keys to move the insertion point to where you want to add a word. Type the new word, then press the space bar on the keyboard.

Removing a word

The insertion point

Delete has been pressed once and the 'y' has been deleted.

The whole word has been removed.

1. To remove a word, use the arrow keys on the keyboard to move the insertion point immediately to the left of the word you want to remove.

2. Once the insertion point is in position, press the Delete key once. The letter immediately to the right of the insertion point disappears.

3. Keep pressing Delete until the whole word has gone. If you want to replace the word you have deleted, just type the new word.

Scrolling

You may not be able to see all of your letter on the screen. If you want to get to a part that you can't see, you'll need to **scroll**. This is the computer word for moving up and down. On the right-hand side of the screen, there's a tiny arrow at the top, pointing up, and one at the bottom, pointing down. Try moving the pointer over the scrolling arrows, and then clicking, to move up or down the page, a little at a time.

Click on this scrolling arrow to move up the letter.

Click here to move down the letter.

Selecting words

These steps show you how to choose, or **select**, a word. When a word is selected, you can remove or replace it. There are many ways to select – you'll come across others later in the book.

The pointer

This word has been selected.

| slowly around, and Maybe one day I'll | slowly around, and Maybe one day I'll | around, and think a day I'll actually vis |

1. To select one word, move the pointer over a word. The pointer may change shape as it moves over the page. When it's over a word, it is an 'I' shape.

2. Press and release the left mouse button twice, very quickly. This is called **double-clicking**. The word appears in white on a black background.

3. To remove the word that you've selected, press the Delete key once. To replace it with another word, just type the new word.

Selecting several words

The pointer was moved from here...

| n France sent me a g me. I think that it m want to travel more | n France sent me a g me. I think that it m want to travel more | e. I think that it may ant to travel more. I |

The pointer

The mouse button was pressed here...   ...and released here.

...to here, where the mouse button was released.

1. Position the pointer immediately to the left of a word. Press and hold down the left mouse button, and **drag** the mouse gently to the right.

2. A black area appears as the pointer is dragged across the words. When you've selected the words you want, release the mouse button.

3. To select words on more than one line, drag the pointer down. If you select too many words, drag the pointer left, then release the mouse button.

Tip

If you've made a mistake, you can **undo** what you've done by holding down the Ctrl key and pressing Z. Alternatively, click on the Undo tool, shown here. It's on the toolbar.

Saving changes

If you have already named and saved a document, you can click on the Save tool at the top of the screen. It has exactly the same effect as pressing Ctrl and S (see page 15). The new version is saved under the document's existing name.

4. Printing onto paper

If you have a printer, you can print out what you've done onto paper. You'll be able to print in color, if you have a color printer.

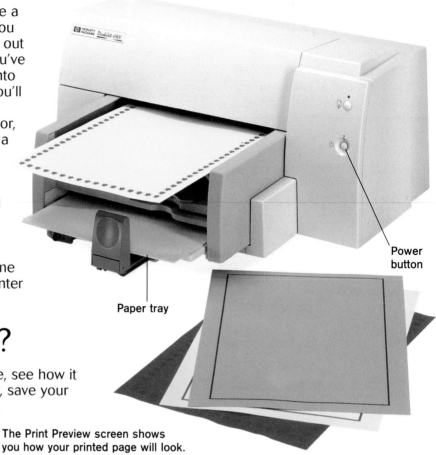

First of all, you need to connect the printer to the system unit, and carefully plug it into the main power supply. Switch on the printer's power button, which is probably on the front, and put some paper in the paper tray, as the printer won't work without paper.

Power button

Paper tray

How will it look?

Before you print what you've done, see how it will look on a piece of paper. First, save your work, then follow the steps below.

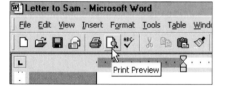

The Print Preview screen shows you how your printed page will look.

1. Your work should still be on the screen. Click on the Print Preview tool, at the top of the screen. A small version of the page appears (see right).

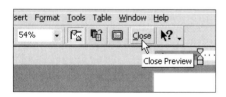

2. Then, return the screen to how it was before you clicked on the Print Preview tool, by clicking on the word Close, near the top of the screen.

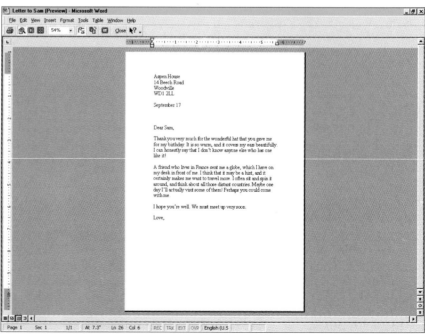

One copy

If you just want to print one copy of your work, there's an easy way to do it. Just move the pointer over the Print tool, which is at the top of the screen, and click. A few moments later, your work will emerge from the printer.

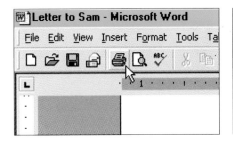

Tip

If your work doesn't print, make sure that the printer is switched on and that there's paper in the paper tray.

Several copies

If you want to print a lot of copies of the same thing, always print one copy first, to check that what you're printing looks right. If it doesn't, make any changes that need to be made, save, then follow these steps.

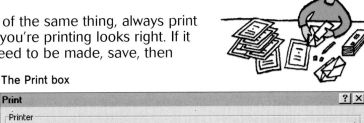

The Print box

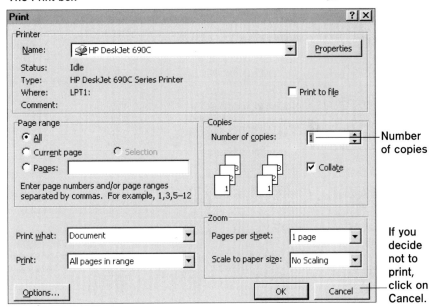

— Number of copies

If you decide not to print, click on Cancel.

1. Move the pointer over File, at the top of the screen, and click. A menu appears. Move the pointer down the menu so that a dark bar is over Print.

2. Click the left mouse button. The Print box appears. Yours should look similar to the one on this page, but Print boxes vary from printer to printer.

3. Type the number of copies you want. The number appears in the box next to Number of copies, on the right-hand side of the Print box.

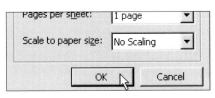

4. Move the pointer over OK (or Print, depending on the printer), and click the mouse button. Several copies of your work will print.

Tip

There's a really quick way to make the Print box appear on the screen, without using the mouse. Hold down the Ctrl key, and press the letter P. The Print box appears.

5. Writing a formal letter

On this page, find out how to write a formal letter, and how to make lettering slightly bigger. Before you start, you need to save, then put away or **close** your Thank you letter, and create a new document. You'll need to do this every time you've finished working on something.

Closing a document

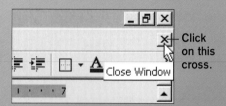

Click on this cross.

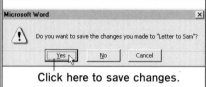

Click here to save changes.

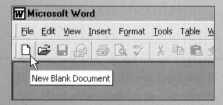

1. Move the pointer over the lower of the two crosses in the top right-hand corner of the screen, and click. If there is only one cross, see page 60.

2. You may see this message. To save any changes you've made, click on Yes. If you don't want to save the changes you've made, click on No.

3. Your letter disappears, and there's no page on the screen. Move the pointer over the New document tool, and click. A new blank document appears.

Starting a new letter

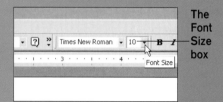

The Font Size box

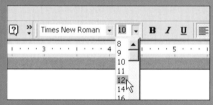

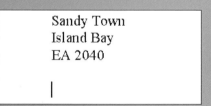

1. Bigger lettering will make the letter easier to read. Move the pointer over the arrow next to the Font Size box, at the top of the screen, and click.

2. A list drops down. Each number is a size of lettering – the higher the number, the bigger the lettering. Move the pointer over 12, and click.

3. Type your name and address, pressing Enter at the end of each line. Then press the Enter key twice, so that a blank line is created under the address.

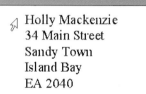

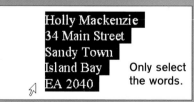

Only select the words.

Click on the arrow.

Then click on this tool.

4. If you'd like to move your name and address to the right-hand side of the page, move the pointer to the left of your name. It changes into an arrow.

5. Now press and hold down the left mouse button, and move the pointer down. When it's level with the bottom line, release the mouse button.

6. Click on the double arrow at the right-hand end of the toolbar. On the menu, click on the Align Right tool. If it's not there, look for it on the toolbar.

Writing the letter

Now that your address is on the right-hand side of the page, you can continue writing the letter. In a formal letter, you need to include the address of the person you're writing to, as well as your own.

1. To keep the words from being selected, press any arrow key. Press the down arrow key until the insertion point moves to the left-hand side of the page.

White Line Tennis Club
Court Lane
Sandy Town
Island Bay
EA 2039

2. Type the name and address of the person you're writing to, then press Enter twice. Type the date, press the Space bar, then press Enter three times.

Dear Mr. Ball,

I would be
about White Line

This line is indented.

3. Type 'Dear ...' and a comma. Press Enter twice. If you want to **indent** the first line, press the Tab key on the keyboard, before you start to type.

Holly Mackenzie
34 Main Street
Sandy Town
Island Bay
EA 2040

(1) Mr. T. Ball
White Line Tennis Club
Court Lane
Sandy Town
Island Bay
EA 2039

(2) March 12, 2000

Dear Mr. Ball,

(3) I would be grateful if you could send me some information about White Line Tennis Club, as I would very much like to play more tennis. Several friends have recommended the W.L.T.C. to me, and I feel that it is time that I became a member of the Club myself.

(4) Please send me details of your membership rates, opening hours and facilities that are available to members. I understand that you also have a swimming pool, which I would like to use, if possible. I look forward to hearing from you soon.

(5) Yours sincerely,

(6) Holly Mackenzie

4. Type the first paragraph, and press Enter twice. Press the Tab key, then type the next paragraph. When the letter is finished, press Enter twice.

5. Type 'Yours sincerely,' if you know the name of the person you're writing to, or 'Kind regards,' if you don't. Then press Enter about four times.

6. Type your name. When the letter is printed onto paper, you can sign in the gap you've left. Save the letter, and print it, if you want. Now close the letter.

6. A letterhead

A letterhead is really just an address at the top of the page, but it's fun to create your own. Follow these steps if you'd like to make one.

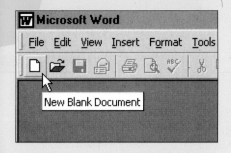

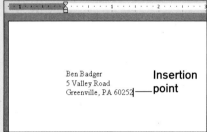

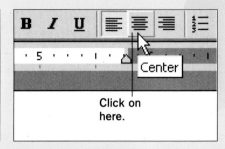

1. First, make sure that you've closed the document you've been working on, as you did on page 20. Now click on the New document tool.

2. At the top of the new document, type your name and address. Remember to press Enter each time you want to start a new line.

3. Using the mouse, select your name and address, as you did on page 20. Now move the pointer over the Center tool shown here, and click.

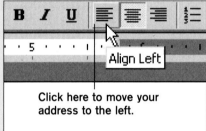

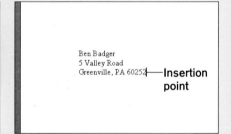

4. Your address moves across to the middle of the page, as shown above. It has uneven edges, because each line is individually centered.

The address on this letterhead has been moved to the left-hand side of the page.

5. If you prefer to have your address on the left, you can move it back, by clicking on the Align Left tool. It will move your address to the left again.

6. Press the down arrow key on the keyboard to keep the words from being selected. This also moves the insertion point to the position shown here.

Ben Badger
5 Valley Road
Greenville, PA 60252

Sophie Kinder
PO Box 471
Pleasant Point
New Town 6015

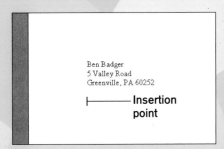

Ben Badger
5 Valley Road
Greenville, PA 60252

├────── Insertion
point

To add a single narrow line, press this key three times.

If you want to add a double line, press this key three times.

Hold down Shift, press this key three times, and then release Shift.

7. Press Enter twice. You can add a straight line that goes across the page, and separates your address from the rest of the letter, if you follow step 8.

8. To add a single, double or thick line under your address, press one of the combinations of keys shown above, and then follow step 9.

9. When you've pressed one of these combinations of keys, you'll see three signs in a row. To change them into a line across the page, press Enter.

Ben Badger
5 Valley Road
Greenville, PA 60252

Ben Badger
5 Valley Road
Greenville, PA 60252

Tip

Instead of using the tools, you can arrange words as you type, using a feature of Word 2000. Move the pointer over the page, so that lines like the ones on the tools appear near it. Double-click, to make the insertion point appear, then start typing. The words are arranged automatically.

10. A line appears. If you'd like to add a different one instead, keep pressing the Backspace key, to remove the line. Now follow steps 8-9 again.

11. Click on the Save tool, and name your letterhead, but don't close it yet. Turn the page, to see how to make the lettering look more interesting.

This address has been moved to the middle of the page, using the Center tool.

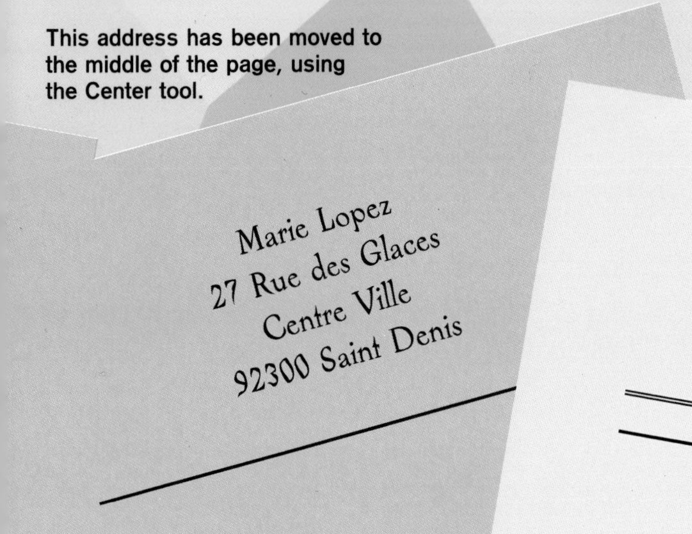

There are different styles of lettering on your computer. Turn the page to find out how to change the style of lettering.

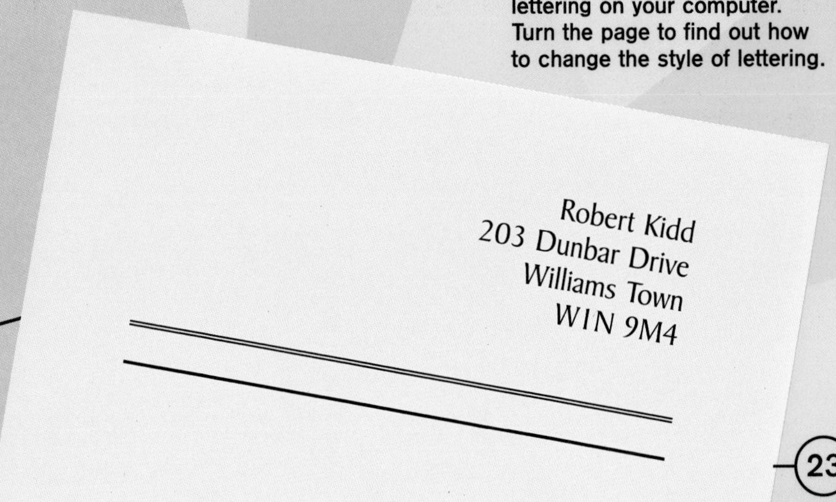

Marie Lopez
27 Rue des Glaces
Centre Ville
92300 Saint Denis

Robert Kidd
203 Dunbar Drive
Williams Town
WIN 9M4

7. Changing the lettering

Bigger lettering

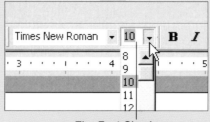

The Font Size box

This letterhead is size 20.

1. Click the mouse to the left of your address and drag across, to select it. Then, click on the arrow next to the Font Size box. A list of lettering sizes appears.

2. Move the pointer over 20, on the list, and click. The lettering becomes bigger. You can make it bigger still, by clicking on a higher number.

Bold and italic lettering

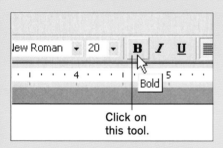

Click on this tool.

Ben Badger
5 Valley Road
Greenville, PA 60252

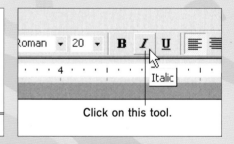

Click on this tool.

1. Select your address, using the mouse as you did before. If you click on this tool, the letters become **thicker**. This is called bold lettering.

2. The tool is like an on/off switch. If you click it again, the letters change back to the way they were. Many of the tools work like this.

3. If you want to see another lettering effect, in which the lettering leans over, *like this*, click on the Italic tool. It's on the toolbar.

Ben Badger
5 Valley Road
Greenville, PA 60252

Ben Badger
5 Valley Road
Greenville, PA 60252

This is Bold and Italic.

Tip

To change the lettering style in part of a document, it's best to select the words using the mouse.

Alternatively, if you want to change all the lettering in a document, hold down the Ctrl key and press A. Everything will be selected.

4. This is called italic lettering. By clicking on the Bold and Italic tools, one after the other, you can make lettering bold and italic at the same time.

5. Save your letterhead when you're happy with the changes you've made, then read the next page, to change the style of the letters themselves.

Differently shaped lettering

At the moment, the lettering style is neat, but not very interesting. Follow these steps to totally transform your page, by changing the style of lettering, or **font**. Your computer may have different fonts from the ones you see in this book.

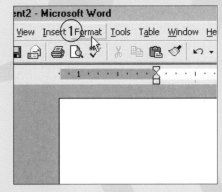

1. Click the mouse button and drag the mouse across your address, to select it. Now move the pointer over Format, at the top of the screen, and click.

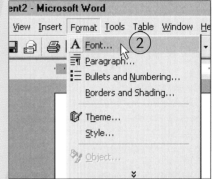

2. A menu drops down. Move the mouse so that a dark bar appears at the top of the menu. When the bar is over Font, click the left mouse button.

3. A large box, called the Font box, appears on the screen. Near the top of the box, the word Font appears three times. Click on the second one down.

4. On the list near the top of the box, there's a dark bar over the name of the font you've been using. In this example, the font is Times New Roman.

5. There are other fonts on the list. Move the pointer over one of them, click, and watch what happens to the writing in the big white Preview area.

6. To see more fonts on the list, click on the tiny scrolling arrows next to the font names. When you've clicked on a font that you like, click on OK.

7. The box disappears, and the lettering looks different. Save, then press the down arrow key until the insertion point will go no further. Start typing a letter.

8. Creating a poster

It's easy to make a small poster, for a concert or a meeting. These pages show you how to arrange words on different lines and how to change the style and size of the lettering.

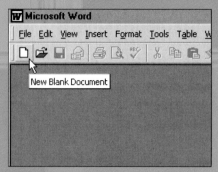

1. First close any documents that are on the screen. Create a new document, by clicking on the New document tool, near the top of the screen.

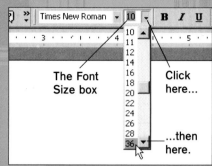

2. Click on the arrow beside the Font Size box. A list of numbers drops down. Click on the tiny down arrow, until you can see 36. Now click on it.

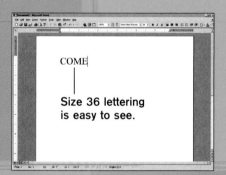

3. Type the first word or two that you want to have on your poster. Then press Enter to start a new line. Type more words, and press Enter again.

4. Each time you press Enter the computer changes the first letter in the line into a capital letter. To change them into little letters, see tip 7 on page 60.

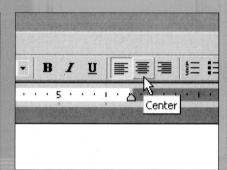

5. Press Ctrl and A, then click on the Center tool, to move the words to the center of the page. Press an arrow key, to keep the words from being selected.

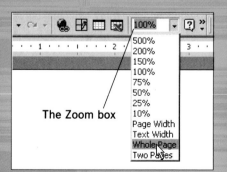

6. Now move the pointer over the arrow next to the Zoom box, and click. A list appears. Move the pointer over 'Whole Page', and click.

7. Your screen changes, and the page is now much smaller. You can see how your poster will look, when it's printed on a sheet of paper.

Tip

If your screen shows a whole page and you want it to look as it usually does, see step 6. Click on the arrow, and then click on 100% on the list.

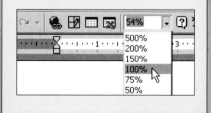

Changing the look

Changing the font can completely change how a poster looks.

These steps show you how to change the style of the lettering and make it bigger, too. You can make your poster look really eye-catching!

1. To change the style of your letters, press Ctrl and A. Then, click on Format on the toolbar at the top of the screen. Click on Font on the menu.

2. The Font box appears. Choose a font style, click on it, then click on OK. Look back at steps 2-7 on page 25 if you've forgotten how to do this.

Select the words using the mouse.

3. To make some words bigger than others, you need to select them first. Drag the mouse across them as you did on page 17.

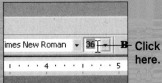

Click here.

4. Click on the Font Size box, on the toolbar. Type a number between 10 (small) and 100 (big), then press Enter. Press any arrow key.

5. Repeat the steps to change any other words or lines of words that you want to change. When you have finished, save your poster.

COME
to a
CONCERT
Doors open at
8:00

IMPORTANT
Meeting
in Room 34
at
10:30
Everyone must
attend

FAIR
JULY
8th-10th
Lots of rides and slides
and food to eat...

9. Adding a page border

Adding a border will make any document look much more eye-catching. Follow these steps if you'd like to add a simple border.

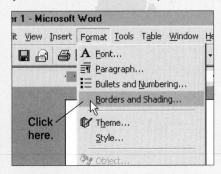

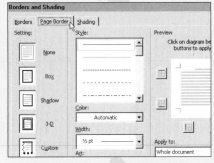

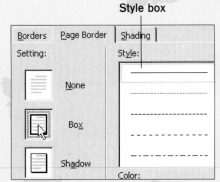
Style box

1. Make sure that you have a document on the screen, then click on Format. On the menu, move the pointer over Borders and Shading, and click.

2. The Borders and Shading box appears. To see the part that you need, move the pointer over Page Border, near the top of the box, and click.

3. To tell the computer to add a page border, move the pointer over the white box next to Box, and click. A rectangle appears in the box when you click.

These examples include different line styles. If you want to try one, click on one of the lines in the Style box (see the picture above step 3).

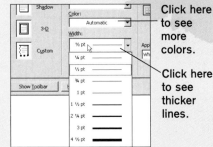
Click here to see more colors.

Click here to see thicker lines.

4. To make a thick colored border, first click on the box below Width. A list of lines appears. Move the pointer onto a thick line, then click.

5. Now click on the box below Color, and click on a color on the list that appears. Click on OK, at the bottom of the box, then save and close.

Tip

To remove a border, repeat steps 1-2 on this page, and then click on the white space next to None. Finally, click on OK.

10. Adding a picture border

On this page, find out how to add a fun border, rather than just a plain one. Word has some borders made up of pictures, and some made up of patterns. If you want to add a fun border to the edge of your document, follow these steps.

1. Make sure that there's a document on your screen, then follow steps 1-3 on page 28. You're now ready to choose which picture border to add.

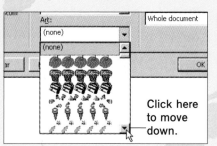

2. Click on the white box under the word Art. A list of small pictures appears. To move up and down the list, click on the tiny arrows beside it.

Click here to move down.

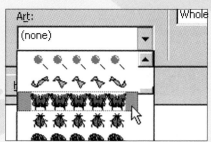

3. Move the pointer down the list until a dark bar moves over a picture or pattern you like. Now click, to choose the picture or pattern.

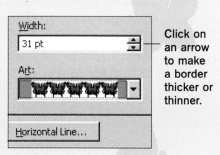

Click on an arrow to make a border thicker or thinner.

4. If you want to make the border thinner, click on the down arrow next to the word Width. To make the border wider, click on the up arrow.

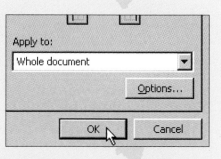

5. When you've chosen a border, click on OK. The box disappears, and a border appears. Save the document, and then close it.

Different borders can change a poster's appearance dramatically.

Don't forget that you'll only be able to print in color if you have a color printer.

11. A numbered list

There are times when it's useful to make a list. On this page, find out how to number a list as you go, and how to add numbering when you've finished writing a list.

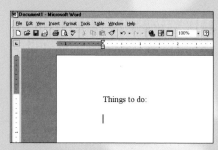

1. Click on the New document tool on the toolbar, to create a new document. Now type a heading, such as 'Things to do:' then press Enter twice.

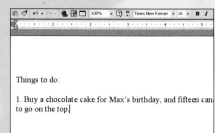

2. Type '1', making sure the period follows immediately after the 1. Press the space bar, and type the first item on the list. It doesn't matter if it's pretty long.

Things to do:

1. Buy a chocolate cake for Max's birthday, and fifteen candles to go on the top.
2. |

The number 2 appears when you press Enter.

3. When you've typed the first item on the list, press Enter. The insertion point moves down a line, and a 2 appears below the 1.

Things to do:

1. Buy a chocolate cake for Max's birthday, and fifteen candles to go on the top.
2. Renew membership to the tennis club.
3. Go to the bank.
4. Write and send letters.
5. Buy this month's music magazine.|

4. Type the other items that need to be on your list. Each time you press Enter, another number appears. Continue until you're finished.

Things to do:

1. Buy a chocolate cake for Max's birthday, and fifteen candles to go on the top.
2. Renew membership to the tennis club.
3. Go to the bank.
4. Write and send letters.
5. Buy this month's music magazine.
6. |

Press Enter to make the 6 disappear.

5. When you've typed the final thing on your list, press Enter. A number appears, so press Enter again, to get rid of it. Now save, and close the list.

Adding numbering later

1. If you write a list, and then decide that you want to add numbers, select all of the words you want in the list, using the mouse.

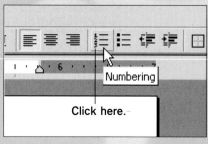

Numbering

Click here.

2. To add numbers, click on this tool, which is the Numbering tool. Numbers appear at the beginning of each new line.

Tip

If you want to make a number disappear from a list, move the insertion point into the line of writing next to the number. Now click on the Numbering tool. The number disappears. To remove all the numbers from a list, select the whole list, and click on the Numbering tool.

12. A 'bulleted' list

When you're making a list, you may prefer to mark the items with small round dots, instead of with numbers. These dots are known as **bullets**. On this page, find out how to add them to a set of directions. First of all, create a new document.

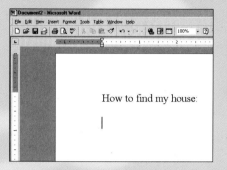

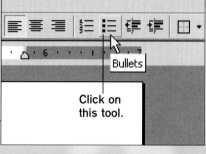

Click on this tool.

1. As before, type a heading, such as 'How to find my house:' and then press Enter twice, to create a blank line before you start the list of directions.

2. Move the pointer over the Bullet tool, shown here. Now click the left mouse button, to make a bullet appear. Type the first instruction on your list.

3. When you've finished typing the first instruction, press Enter. The insertion point moves down a line, and a second bullet appears below the first.

This is a bulleted list. The bullets draw attention to each point. Find out how to make fun bullets on page 32.

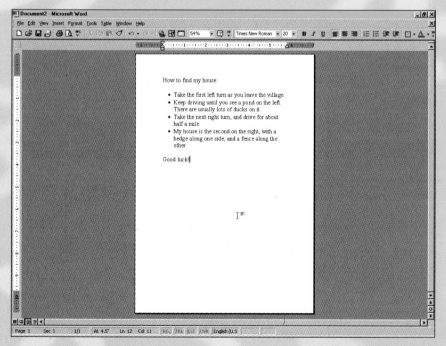

If you want to see your whole list on the screen, and can't remember how to do this, turn to page 26.

4. Add as many instructions as you need. When you've typed the last instruction, press Enter. A bullet appears, so press Enter, to make it disappear.

- My house is the second on the right, hedge along one side, and a fence al other.

Good luck!

5. Type a 'Good luck!' message if you don't have much faith in your own directions. Now save the list, if you want to keep it for another time, and close it.

13. A fun list

When you've created a bulleted list, as you did on page 31, you can change the bullets into little symbols. Create a bulleted list, or follow the steps on page 56 to open one that you saved earlier.

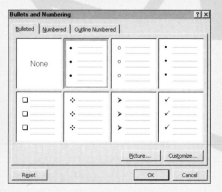

The Bullets and Numbering box

Click on a bullet style.

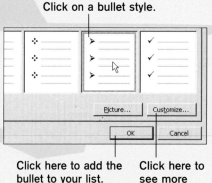

Click here to add the bullet to your list.

Click here to see more bullet styles.

Click here to choose a new bullet style.

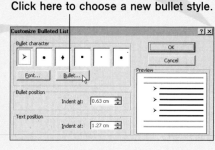

The Customize Bulleted List box

1. Using the mouse, select the list. Click on Format, at the top of the screen, and on Bullets and Numbering. The Bullets and Numbering box appears.

2. You'll see different bullet styles in the box. Click on one, then click on OK if you want to add it to your list. To choose another, click on Customize.

3. The Customize Bulleted List box appears, with bullet styles at the top. To create your own bullet, click on Bullet, which is next to Font.

The Symbol box

Click here to see more fonts with symbols.

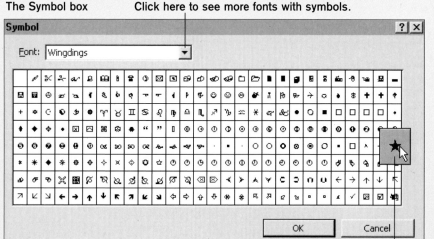

Click on a symbol to see it more clearly.

4. The Symbol box appears (see left). It is filled with tiny symbols arranged in a grid. Try clicking on one, to see a larger version of it.

5. To see other fonts that contain symbols, click on the arrow to the right of Font. Click on a font, and you'll see different symbols in the grid.

6. Click on a symbol, then click on OK. When the Customize box reappears, click on OK. The bullets change. Press any arrow key, then save and close.

If you'd like to add a page border, turn to pages 28-29.

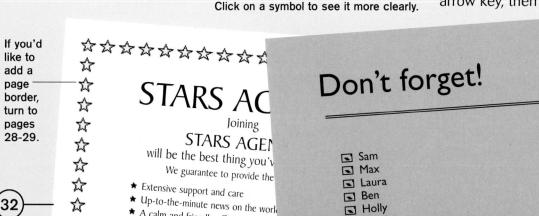

Don't forget!

14. Extra effects

On this page, find out how to add extra effects that will make a document look even better.

Shadows and outlines

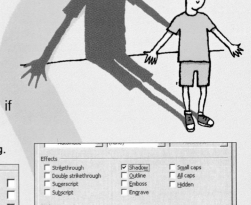

There are lots of writing effects available in the Font box. You'll find they look better if you're using big writing, so see page 24 if you've forgotten how to change the size of your lettering.

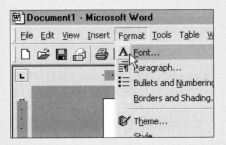

Click here to create shadowy writing.

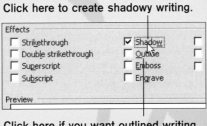

Click here if you want outlined writing.

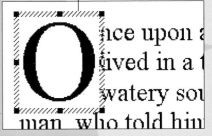

1. Make sure that a document is open, with some lettering in it. Select the lettering you want to change, using the mouse. Click on Format, then on Font.

2. The Font box appears. Under the Effects heading are different writing effects. Try clicking on Shadow, so that a checkmark appears next to it.

3. In the big white area, you'll see what the effect looks like. Click on OK, to add the effect that you have chosen, then save. Press any arrow key.

Here are some of the writing effects that are available in the Font box.

Shadow   Outline   Emboss   Engrave

Giant first letters

In some books, new chapters start with a giant first letter, which is called a drop capital. Click on the New document tool and follow these steps.

Press any arrow key to remove this box.

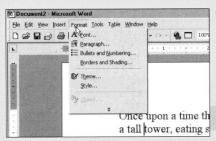

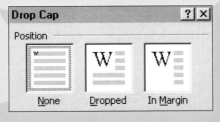

This is the top part of the Drop Cap box.

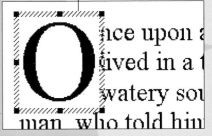

1. First type a paragraph. Using the arrow keys, move the insertion point anywhere within the paragraph. Click on Format. A menu drops down.

2. Now click on the arrows at the bottom of the menu. The menu becomes longer. Click on Drop Cap. The Drop Cap box appears.

3. Click on the middle box, above Dropped, then on OK. The first letter in the paragraph changes into a drop capital. Press any arrow key, then save.

15. Adding headings

On the next few pages, find out how to organize and improve long documents. Clear headings and section headings make a long document easier to read, and numbered pages (see page 36) help you stay organized.

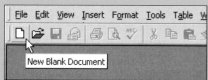

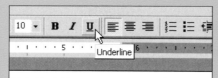

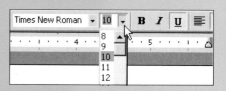

1. Create a new document, type the words that you want to include in your heading, and press Enter twice. Now type an introduction.

2. To select the heading, move the pointer to the left of the heading, and click. Now click on the Center tool (see page 22) and on the Underline tool.

3. To make the heading bigger than the rest of the writing, click on the arrow next to the Font Size box. On the list, click on a bigger number.

4. Using the arrow keys, move the pointer to the end of the introduction. Press Enter twice, then type a section heading and press Enter again.

5. Save what you've done so far, then type the information you want to have under this section heading. You may want several paragraphs.

6. Using the mouse, select the section heading. Click on the Underline tool, or the Bold tool, or both, depending on how you want the heading to look.

7. Save again, then repeat steps 4-6, until you've created as many section headings and sections as you want. Now save the document again.

In this example, the section headings are in different styles, to show you how different effects look.

and other plants...

after

ut

Birds of the World

There are lots of amazing birds that live in different countries around the world. Here are a few of the most extraordinary ones:

Penguins
Penguins are sea birds that cannot fly. They all live in the southern half of the world and seven species live in the Antarctic. Penguins are kept warm by two layers of short, tightly-packed feathers and by a layer of fat under their skin. Although they cannot fly, penguins are very good swimmers and divers. They use their stiff, narrow wings as flippers in the water, and often come flying out of the water to take a breath. On sloping ground, penguins slide along on their fronts, pushing themselves forward with their flippers.

Hummingbirds
Hummingbirds are named after the sound their wings make when they fly. To eat, they poke their beaks into flowers and suck up the nectar through their tube-like tongues. Hummingbirds can hover in one place, by moving their wings backward and forward, up to 3,000 times a minute.

Ostriches
Ostriches live in African grasslands. They are the biggest birds in the world and can be up to 2.5m (8ft.) tall – taller than a horse. Ostriches cannot fly, but they can run very fast to escape from predators. They feed mainly on grass

This heading is underlined.

Bold headings stand out from other lettering.

A heading that is both bold and underlined is easy to see.

Tip

Each time you reach the bottom of a page, a new one appears, and the screen looks as if it's split into two parts. Don't worry – you can just continue typing.

16. Moving and copying

If you discover that some information is in the wrong place, or you want to copy something from one place to another, don't despair. You don't need to type it again – it's quick and easy to move and **copy** sections. In Microsoft® Word 2000 you can 'collect' several sections and then choose which section to put where. First follow the steps on this page, then turn to page 58, to find out about moving and copying several sections.

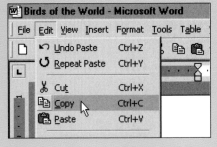

1. Using the mouse, select the section you want to move or copy. Click at the beginning of the section, drag down the side, then release the mouse button.

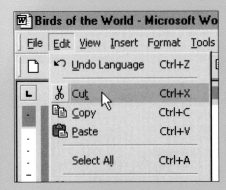

2. To move the section, you need to **cut**, or remove it. Click on Edit, and then on Cut. The section disappears. Now follow steps 3 and 4.

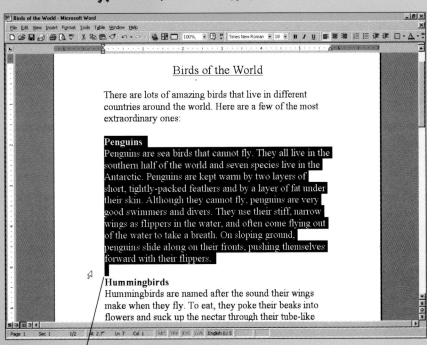

Once a section has been selected, it can be cut or copied, and then pasted somewhere else.

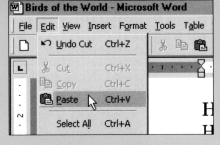

The insertion point

3. When you **paste** a section, it appears by the insertion point. Using the arrow keys, move the insertion point to where you want to paste the section.

4. To make the section appear, click on Edit, and then on Paste. The section appears in its new position. Now save the changes you've made.

5. To copy a selected section, click on Edit, then on Copy. Now follow steps 3 and 4 to paste the copied section where you want it. Save the changes.

17. Numbering pages

You can make page numbers appear on each page when you print, but this only makes sense if there's more than one page in your document. Make sure that you've got a document with more than one page on your screen. If you saved one earlier, then closed it, turn to page 56, to find out how to work on it again.

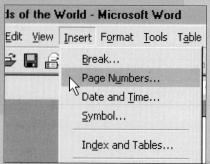

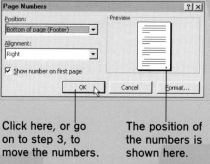

Click here to change the position of the numbers.

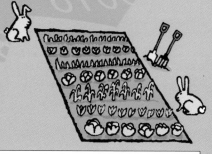

Click here, or go on to step 3, to move the numbers.

The position of the numbers is shown here.

1. Click on Insert, so that a menu appears. Using the mouse, move the pointer down the menu until a dark bar is over Page Numbers, then click.

2. This box appears. If you're happy to have page numbers in the bottom right-hand corner of each page, move the pointer over OK, and click.

3. To have numbers in the middle, or on the left, click on the box below Alignment. Click on the option that you prefer, then click on OK. Now save.

18. Neat edges

You've used the Align Left, Center and Align Right tools to move words across the page, but you haven't yet used the **Justify** tool, which is next to them on the toolbar. This tool arranges the words so that each line is the same length. Read on, to find out how to make paragraphs look clean by justifying them.

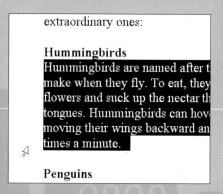

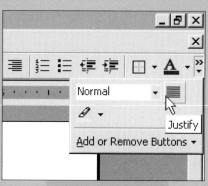

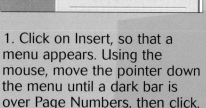

1. Using the mouse, select the section that you want to change, as you did on page 20. You don't need to select the section heading.

2. Click on the double arrow at the right-hand end of the toolbar. On the menu, click on the Justify tool. If it's not there, look for it on the toolbar.

3. This paragraph is justified and neat, with a straight right-hand edge. Press an arrow key, to keep the paragraph from being selected. Now save.

19. A heading on every page

As well as adding numbers, you can add headings to every page. These are called **headers**, in computer jargon, but they have nothing to do with soccer! Once you've set them up, they'll appear on every new page. You need to have a document open.

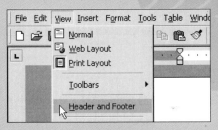

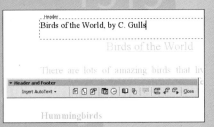

1. Move the pointer over the word View, and click, so that a menu appears. Move the dark bar over Header and Footer, and click the left mouse button.

2. A Header area appears, with a dotted line around it. At the same time, the Header and Footer toolbar appears, and your writing becomes pale.

3. There is a flashing insertion point in the Header area. Type the words that you'd like to have as a header on every page of the document.

Align Right

4. You can move the header to the right-hand side of the page, if you prefer. To do this, you just need to click on the Align Right tool.

The header looks lighter, to distinguish it from the other writing.

> Birds of the World, by C. Gulls
>
> Birds of the World

5. Click on Close at the right end of the Header toolbar. The toolbar disappears and the header appears at the top of the page. Save and then close.

The header appears on every page.

Header

Birds of the World, by C. Gulls

Birds of the World

There are lots of amazing birds that live in different countries around the world. Here are a few of the most extraordinary ones:

Hummingbirds
Hummingbirds are named after the sound their wings make when they fly. To eat, they poke their beaks into flowers and suck up the nectar through their tube-like tongues. Hummingbirds can hover in one place, by moving their wings backward and forward, up to 3,000 times a minute.

Penguins
Penguins are sea birds that cannot fly. They all live in the southern half of the world and seven species live in the Antarctic. Penguins are kept warm by two layers of short, tightly-packed feathers and by a layer of fat under their skin. Although they cannot fly, penguins are very good swimmers and divers. They use their stiff, narrow wings as flippers in the water, and often come flying out of the water to take a breath. On sloping ground, penguins slide along on their fronts, pushing themselves forward with their flippers.

Ostriches
Ostriches live in African grasslands. They are the biggest birds in the world and can be up to 2.5m (8ft.) tall – taller than a horse. Ostriches cannot fly, but they can run very fast to escape from predators. They feed mainly on grass and other plants. Both the males and the females look after the chicks.

1

...World, by C. Gulls

...out of lots of ...fferent shapes ...t is the male ...down from ...ng to attract ..t, the male

The writing on these pages is justified.

Tip

You can still make changes when you've closed the header. Just double-click on it, and make the changes.

20. Checking your spelling

There are two ways to check your spelling. You can check a whole document at once, by following the steps on this page. Also, you can use the lines like snakes, which appear under words that the computer thinks are misspelled. The computer can check your grammar too, but it's not as useful as the spelling check. If you removed the 'snakes' on page 12 and want them back, follow the steps on page 39. Or, you could always check your own spelling and change words yourself, like you did on pages 16-17! Make sure no words are selected, or you'll confuse the computer.

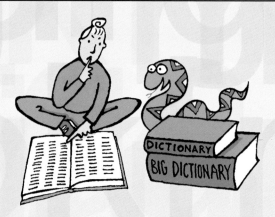

Checking the whole document

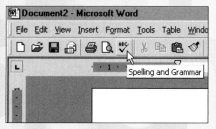

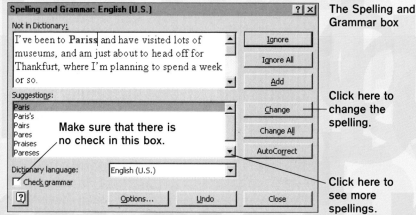

Make sure that there is no check in this box.

The Spelling and Grammar box

Click here to change the spelling.

Click here to see more spellings.

1. To check the spelling of all the words in your document, click on the Spelling and Grammar tool. The Spelling and Grammar box appears.

2. Now you need to remove the grammar check, as it can be confusing. Click on Check grammar, so that there is no checkmark in the box next to it.

3. Near the top of the box, your first spelling mistake is shown. Under Suggestions, there are alternative spellings, if the computer can suggest any.

4. To replace the word with a word on the list, click once on the replacement word so that a dark bar appears over it. Now click on Change.

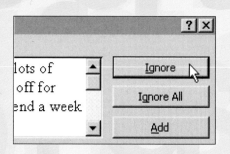

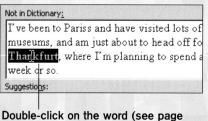

Double-click on the word (see page 17), then type the spelling you want.

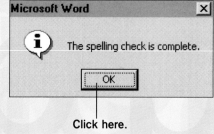

The spelling check is complete.

Click here.

5. If none of the words on the list are the word or the spelling that you want, click on Ignore. You may need to correct the word yourself, later.

6. A second mistake appears. Correct it by choosing a word on the list, or just double-click on it, type the correct spelling, and then click on Change.

7. Check the whole document. When you get to the end, you'll see this message. Click on OK, then save any changes you've made, and close the document.

Weird spellings

As you check your spelling, you'll find that the computer makes some very strange suggestions, which aren't always right. Although it can recognize lots of words, it can't recognize every word you use. It often suggests funny alternatives to names. Try typing in some of your friends' names, and see what it comes up with!

Choosing and using 'snakes'

Click here.

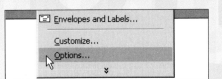

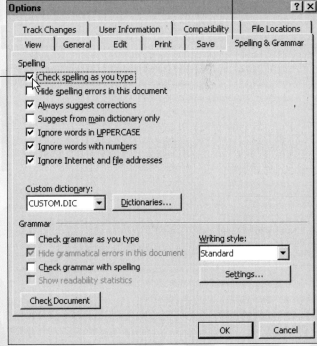

1. To make the 'snakes' appear, click on Tools, at the top of the screen. Move the pointer down the menu, until the dark bar is over Options, and click.

2. The Options box appears on the screen (see right). To see the part of it that you need to use, click on Spelling and Grammar, at the top of the box.

3. Click on the box next to Check spelling as you type, so that a check appears. Now click on OK, to make 'snakes' appear under misspelled words.

Click here so that a check appears in the box. Red 'snakes' will appear under misspelled words.

The Options box allows you to tell the computer whether you want the 'snakes' or not.

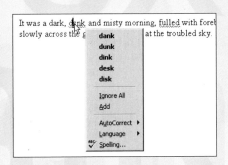

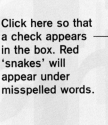

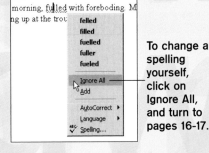

To change a spelling yourself, click on Ignore All, and turn to pages 16-17.

4. Move the pointer over a word with a red 'snake' under it, and click the <u>right</u> mouse button once. A menu showing alternative spellings appears.

5. If there's a spelling that looks correct, click on it. The menu and the 'snake' vanish, and the word is replaced by the spelling you've chosen.

6. If you don't want to choose any of the options, click on Ignore All. The menu and the 'snake' disappear, and the word stays as it was. Save and close.

21. Writing your resume

Imagine that you're applying for your ideal job or work experience. You need a resume, which shows your interests and qualifications. You can create your own resume, by setting up a framework (a Microsoft® Word 2000 table), and filling it in. Look at the example on the next page for some ideas, and don't forget to check your spelling (see pages 38-39) – you don't want to leave in any mistakes!

Setting up a framework

Before you can set up a framework, you need to create a new document, so click on the New document tool. Then follow the steps, to create a framework that you can type in.

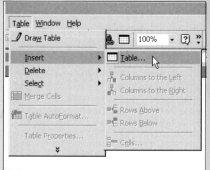

1. Type 'RESUME' and press Enter twice. Click on Table, and on Insert. On the second menu, the word Table appears again. Click on it.

Type 2 here, then press Tab.

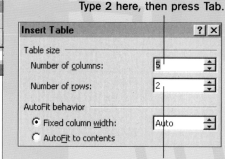

Type 9 here, then click on OK.

2. The Insert Table box appears. Type 2 in the Number of **columns** box, press the Tab key, then type 9 in the Number of **rows** box. Now click on OK.

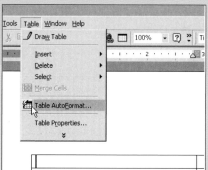

3. A table appears. It is made up of boxes called **cells**. To make the table invisible when it's printed, click on Table, then on Table AutoFormat.

Click here. **This shows how the table will look when it is printed.**

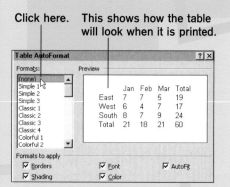

4. The Table AutoFormat box appears. Click on (none) in the top left-hand corner, so that the lines disappear from the white area on the right. Click on OK.

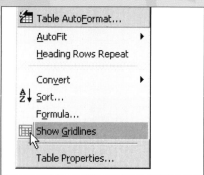

5. If the table disappears, click on Table, and on the arrows at the bottom of the menu. Click on Show Gridlines, and a pale version of the table appears.

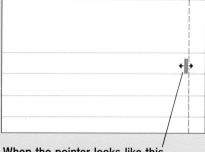

When the pointer looks like this, move the line about 1 in. to the left.

6. Move the pointer over the line between the two columns. Hold down the mouse button, and drag the mouse a little to the left. Release the button.

Using the framework

The framework is now ready for you to type in your details. Just follow these steps, to create your personal resume.

The table is a pale framework of cells.

1. Use the arrow keys to move the insertion point into the first cell. Type 'Name:' and press Tab, to move the insertion point to the cell on the right.

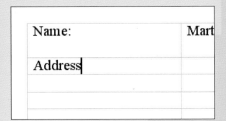

Press Enter to start a new line within a cell, or to create a blank line.

2. Type your name, and press Enter. This creates a blank line between categories. Press Tab, to move to the next cell, type the next category, and continue.

3. If you type an **e-mail** address, it may become blue and underlined. If this happens, press the Backspace key once, before you do anything else.

RESUME

Name:	Martin Mills
Address:	140 Riverside Road Tulsa, OK 74113
Phone:	(918) 622-8914
E-mail address:	Martin.Mills@Usborne.co.uk
Education:	Riverside High School, Tulsa OK River Town College, Oklahoma City OK
Qualifications:	B.A. Business Administration and Computer Science Minors in Math and Art Graduated Summa Cum Laude
Work Experience:	1992-present: Sales Associate at Duffs 1989-1992: Sales Manager at Arden Shoes 1985-1989: Sales Assistant at Ferguson and Company
Interests:	Playing soccer Going to movies Reading

4. Type in all of the information that you want to include, then check for spelling mistakes (see pages 38-39). Finally, save and close your resume.

Tip

To add an extra row to the bottom of a table, move the insertion point into the bottom right-hand cell, using the arrow keys. Press the Tab key, and a new row appears.

22. A logo letterhead

On these pages, you can find out how to make a letterhead that includes a little picture, or symbol. You can add symbols to all kinds of different documents, and here a symbol has been added to a letterhead, to make the letterhead look more interesting.

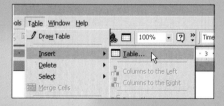

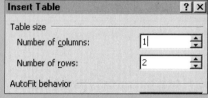

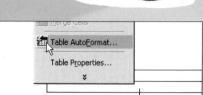

The table is made up of two long cells.

1. Click on the New document tool. Click on Table, at the top of the screen, then on Insert. On the second menu, the word Table appears again. Click on it.

2. The Insert Table box pops up. To create a table, type 1 in the columns box, press the Tab key, and then type 2 in the rows box. Click on OK.

3. A long table appears. To make the table invisible when it is printed on paper, click on Table, and then on Table AutoFormat, on the menu.

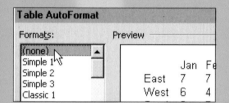

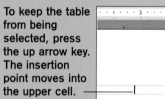

To keep the table from being selected, press the up arrow key. The insertion point moves into the upper cell.

4. The Table AutoFormat box appears. Click on (none), and then click on OK. If the table disappears, follow step 5 on page 40. A pale table appears.

5. Press Ctrl and A, to select everything, then click on the Center tool. Press the up arrow key, to move the insertion point into the upper cell.

6. Click on Insert, then click on Symbol, and wait a moment. You'll see the Symbol box, shown below left, filled with lots of little symbols.

7. If Wingdings isn't next to Font, click on the arrow. A list appears, and you can move up or down it by clicking on the tiny arrows. Find Wingdings.

8. Now click on Wingdings. Other symbols appear, but they're small and hard to see. If you click on any one, you'll see a larger version of it.

9. Click on different symbols in the grid, until you find one that you like. Click on Insert, at the bottom of the box, and then click on Close, next to it.

This is the Symbol box

Click here to see a list of fonts.

Click here if the box doesn't look like this.

Click on a symbol to see it more clearly.

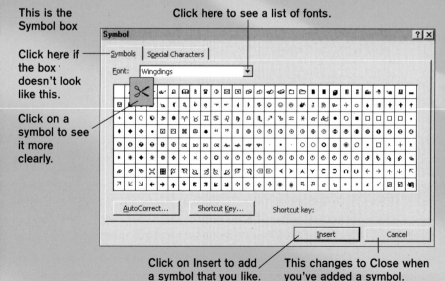

Click on Insert to add a symbol that you like.

This changes to Close when you've added a symbol.

The Font Size box

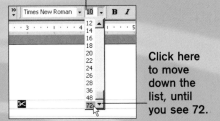

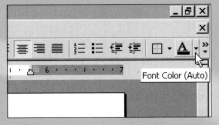

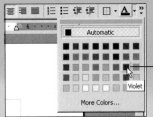

Choose a color by clicking on a square in the box.

10. The symbol is very small, so select it, using the mouse. Click on the arrow next to the Font Size box, and on the down arrow, until you see 72.

11. Click on the number 72. The symbol becomes larger. Now click on the arrow next to the Font Color tool, at the top of the screen.

12. A box filled with different colors drops down. Move the pointer over a color you like, and click, to make your symbol this color. The box vanishes.

To see the correct color, press an arrow key.

Snips Hair Salon
42 High Street
Bla

Click here to move the insertion point to the left of the page.

13. Your symbol will not be the color you chose until you keep it from being selected. Press an arrow key on the keyboard, to see the correct color.

14. Press the down arrow key to move the insertion point into the lower cell, then type your address. Press Enter each time you want to start a new line.

15. Press the down arrow key, until the insertion point is below the table. Click on the Align Left tool, to move the insertion point to the left, then save and close.

If you want to change how your address looks, you could select it, and change its font (see page 25).

This symbol is from a font called Webdings. You may have it on your list of fonts.

Remember that you'll only be able to print your letterhead in color if you have a color printer.

Snips Hair Salon
42 High Street
Bladeley
MA 4601

To all of our regular customers:

As you may know, we have recently taken on two new members of staff, and are now able to see many more customers each day.

To celebrate, we are offering all of our regular customers a 10% discount on their next hair ... hope that all of you will make an

ark Apartments
entral Street
l City, CA 90001

4-3-2000

ng a great time staying
City. They are right in
nd it's really easy to

y, and saw the
oked so funny.

Sarah Star
15 Sun Street
Sky Town
SK4 2TW

Thursday

he lovely hot weather. I've just
cal pool, and feel very refreshed.
the same for my plants - they
really must water them a little.

en very busy, helping to set up
aturday. The hall looks
en added

23. An alphabetical phone list

You may keep your friends' phone numbers in a book, or on scattered pieces of paper, but you'd probably find it useful to have a handy list, right by the phone. Follow these steps, to create a list, and to put the names in alphabetical order.

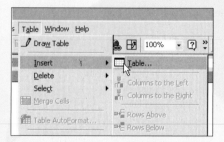

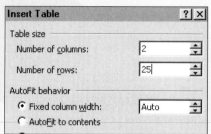

The Font Size box.
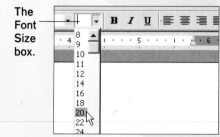

1. Click on the New document tool. Then click on Table, and on Insert, on the menu. On the second menu, the word Table appears again. Click on it.

2. The Insert table box pops up. Type 2 in the columns box, and press Tab. In the rows box, type 25, then click on OK. A table appears on the screen.

3. Select the table by pressing the Ctrl key and the letter A. Click on the arrow next to the Font Size box, and then on 20, on the list that drops down.

Tables are made up of boxes, which are called cells.

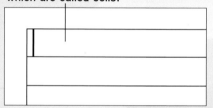

Name	Phone Num

You might see this square. It appears when the pointer is over a table.

Name	Phon
Max	

4. To keep the table from being selected, press an arrow key. Using the arrow keys, move the insertion point into the cell in the top left-hand corner.

5. Type 'Name', and press Enter, to make the cell bigger. Press Tab, on the keyboard, to move to the cell on the right. Type 'Phone Number', and press Tab.

6. The insertion point moves to the left-hand cell on the next line. Type the name of one of your friends, and press Tab, to move to the cell on the right.

A line of cells going down is a column.

Name	Phone Number
Max	542-3219

A line of cells going across is a row.

(432) 582-3688
342-451-7980
981-2205
(020) 8744 6429
421-904-3635
185691

When the insertion point is here, press Tab to add a row.

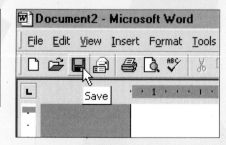

7. In the right-hand cell, type your friend's phone number. Now press Tab, so that the insertion point moves down to the next line, or row.

8. Add as many names and numbers as you want. If you need to add a row, move the insertion point into the last cell, and press Tab.

9. Save what you've done so far, and then move onto the next page to find out how to put the phone list in alphabetical order.

Alphabetical order

Move the pointer next to the first name, so that you don't select the heading.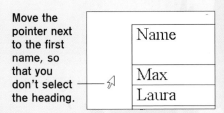

1. To select the items that you want to put into alphabetical order, first move the pointer into the white area to the left of the first name.

Move the pointer down until it is to the left of the bottom name.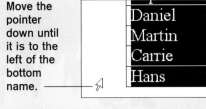

2. Press and hold down the left mouse button, and move the pointer down the list, until it's level with the bottom name. Now release the mouse button.

3. The list is selected. To put it into alphabetical order, click on Table. Click on the arrows at the bottom of the menu, to see more options. Click on Sort.

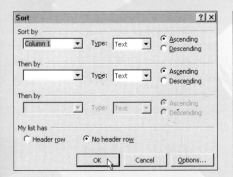

4. The Sort box appears on the screen. You don't need to change anything in the box – just click on OK to tell the computer to sort your list.

5. The items are arranged in alphabetical order. Press an arrow key, so that the table is no longer selected. Save the changes, and close the list.

You can also sort items that aren't in a table – just select the items you want to sort, and follow steps 3 and 4 on this page.

Tips

1. You can move the insertion point around a table, using the arrow keys. You can also move it using the mouse – just move the pointer to where you want the insertion point, and click.

2. To remove a row, move the insertion point into the row. Click on Table on the toolbar, on Delete on the menu, and on Rows. The row disappears.

If you'd like to add a border to the edge of the page, follow the instructions on pages 28-29.

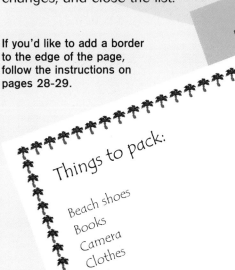

24. Managing your accounts

It's sometimes hard to keep track of how much you've spent in a week, and you might find it helpful to have a simple system. If you create a table in Microsoft® Word 2000, you can type in how much you've spent each day, and then get the computer to add up the totals at the end of the week. Just follow these steps.

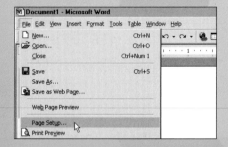

1. Click on the New document tool to create a new document. Now click on File, at the top of the screen, then on Page Setup, on the menu.

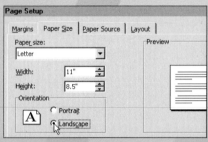

2. When the Page Setup box appears, click on Paper Size, at the top. Click on the word Landscape, or on the circle next to it, then click on OK.

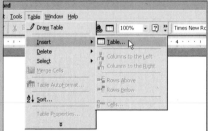

3. Click on Table, at the top of the screen, and then on Insert. On the second menu, the word Table appears again. Click on it. The Insert Table box appears.

Insert Table

Table size	
Number of columns:	6
Number of rows:	9

AutoFit behavior
Fixed column width: Auto

4. Type the number 6 into the columns box and press Tab, to move to the rows box. Type the number 9, and click on OK. A table appears on your screen.

Click here. ——14

5. Press Ctrl and A, to select the table, then click on the arrow next to the Font Size box. On the list, move the pointer over 14, and click.

The insertion point is in the top left-hand cell.

6. Press an arrow key, to keep the table from being selected, then move the insertion point to the cell in the top left-hand corner of the table.

Press the Tab key on the keyboard to move from cell to cell.

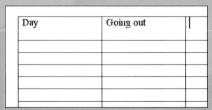

Day	Going out	

7. Type 'Day', press Enter, then press the Tab key, to move one cell to the right. Type the name of something you spend money on, then press Tab.

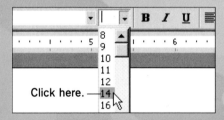

Savings		

8. In the next three cells to the right, type other categories of spending. Your categories may not be the same as the ones shown here. Now press Tab.

Daily total	

9. In the last cell in this line, or row, type 'Daily total', then press the Tab key, to move to the next row of cells. Now save what you've done so far.

If part of the table moves off the screen, you can see it again by clicking on the scrolling arrows (see the big picture on page 47).

10. In the first cell in the second row, type 'Monday'. Now press Tab, and in the next cell, type your first amount, such as 5.25.

11. Press Tab, and fill in what you've spent in each category. Make sure that you always type the amounts in the same way, such as 0.37, rather than 37.

12. Move the insertion point into the last cell in the row, and then click on Table. Click on the arrows at the bottom of the menu, and on Formula.

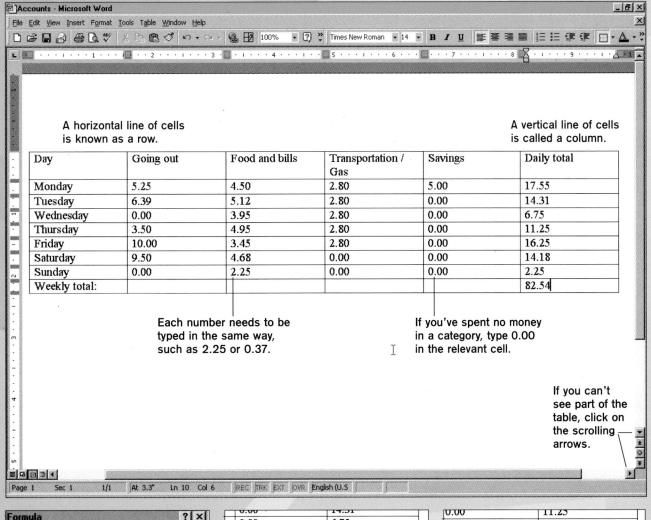

A horizontal line of cells is known as a row.

A vertical line of cells is called a column.

Day	Going out	Food and bills	Transportation / Gas	Savings	Daily total
Monday	5.25	4.50	2.80	5.00	17.55
Tuesday	6.39	5.12	2.80	0.00	14.31
Wednesday	0.00	3.95	2.80	0.00	6.75
Thursday	3.50	4.95	2.80	0.00	11.25
Friday	10.00	3.45	2.80	0.00	16.25
Saturday	9.50	4.68	0.00	0.00	14.18
Sunday	0.00	2.25	0.00	0.00	2.25
Weekly total:					82.54

Each number needs to be typed in the same way, such as 2.25 or 0.37.

If you've spent no money in a category, type 0.00 in the relevant cell.

If you can't see part of the table, click on the scrolling arrows.

Formula

Formula:

=SUM(LEFT)

Number format:

Press the Shift key and 9, or the Shift key and 0, to type the brackets.

The weekly total appears in the cell.

13. The Formula box appears. Press the Backspace key on the keyboard until you've emptied the upper box. Now type =SUM(LEFT) into the box.

14. Now click on OK, and the total spent on Monday appears. When you've filled in the other days, move the insertion point into the bottom right-hand cell.

15. Click on Table, and then on Formula. In the top box, you'll see =SUM(ABOVE). Click on OK, to find out the weekly total. Save and close the document.

47

25. Using pictures

Despite its name, Microsoft® Word 2000 isn't just about words – you can also add pictures to a document. On these pages, you can find out how to add a picture to a blank document. Turn to pages 50-51, to find out how to combine pictures and words.

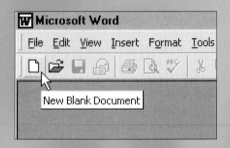

1. Click on the New document tool. Move the pointer to where you want the picture to appear. Double-click, and the insertion point appears.

2. Now click on Insert, at the top of the screen. Move the pointer over Picture. A second menu appears. Move the pointer over Clip Art, and click.

3. The Insert ClipArt box appears. Click on Pictures, near the top of the box. The names of categories appear in the main part of the box.

4. If you want to see more categories, click on the tiny down arrow on the right-hand side of the box. Now click on a category, such as Cartoons.

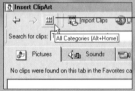

Click here to return to the category names at any time.

If the box doesn't look like this, click here.

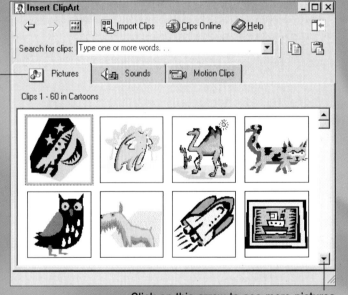

The Insert ClipArt box.

Click on this arrow to see more pictures.

5. After a moment, pictures should appear. If they don't, click on the All Categories tool. The category names reappear. Now try another category.

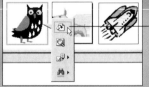

Click here to add the picture.

6. To add a picture to your document, click on it. A menu of signs appears. Move the pointer over the top sign, and click. (See Tip 2.)

Tip

1. When you click on Clip Art (see step 2), you may see a box that tells you that the computer needs to add pictures. Click on OK, then wait a few moments.

2. If you see a box that tells you that the picture you have chosen is stored on a disc, or CD-ROM, see the section 'Using a CD-ROM' on page 49.

Find out how to make a picture bigger on page 50.

Press Enter
to move the
insertion
point below
the picture.

You can add a message to a picture.

7. A picture appears, but it may be hidden behind the Insert ClipArt box. Just click on the cross in the top right-hand corner of the box, to close it.

8. To type below the picture, press Enter. Or, to type somewhere else, move the pointer to where you want to type, and double-click.

Using a CD-ROM

When you click on Insert, you may see a message instead of a picture. If this happens, don't worry — some pictures are stored on the CD-ROM that Microsoft® Word 2000 came on. Find this CD-ROM, then follow these steps to add the picture.

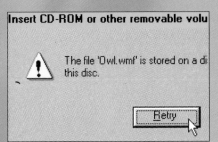

Happy Birtho

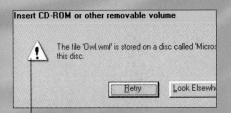

Insert CD-ROM or other removable volume

⚠ The file 'Owl.wmf' is stored on a disc called 'Micros
this disc.

[Retry]   Look Elsewh

This symbol tells you
that there is a problem.

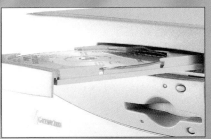

Insert CD-ROM or other removable volu

⚠ The file 'Owl.wmf' is stored on a di
this disc.

[Retry]

1. You'll see this message if the picture is on the CD-ROM. Find the CD-ROM drive on the system unit (see page 4), and press the button next to it.

2. A drawer slides out from the drive. Place the CD-ROM in the drawer, with the writing facing up. Now press the button again, to move the drawer back in.

3. Wait a while, until the CD-ROM stops whirring, then click on Retry. The picture appears on the screen. Remove the CD-ROM from the drive.

26. Pictures with words

Here you can find out how to combine words and pictures, and how to change the size of a picture. Big pictures sometimes push writing, or themselves, off the page, so watch out – you may need to make pictures smaller.

You can also find out how to make words flow, or **wrap**, around a picture. This works better if there's a lot of writing on the page.

A picture border can make a page look even better. Find out how to add one on page 29.

Find out how to add a heading to every page on page 37.

1. Create a new document, then type some words. Press Enter three times, leaving a space. This is where you'll add a picture.

2. Type any other writing you want to include, and save. Using the up arrow key, move the insertion point into the space you left for the picture.

3. Follow the steps on pages 48-49, to add a picture. If the picture is very big, follow the steps below, to make it smaller. Save what you've done so far.

Up, up and away!

Yesterday was amazing! We went to Space Center and found out all abo the space shuttle. The buildings we huge and we saw the quarters tha astronauts live in when they're in space – they're really small. The thing of all was touching a piece the Moon, but I really liked the shop, too. I bought a T-shirt wi picture of the shuttle on it, as

It must be very strange being have to eat weird food and a space for ages. Seeing the u must be incredible, though. I'd really like to do.

A Desert Adventure

A Desert Adventure, by Sandy Dune

In a desert far from here, there lives a camel who lives in a cave. He doesn't do very much; he just eats and sleeps, and visits his friends. Occasionally he goes for a little walk around that part of the desert, but mostly he just sits. However, it wasn't always like this.

Some years ago, when he was quite a bit younger than he is now, the camel decided that he was bored with eating and sleeping and visiting his friends. He wanted to have an adventure, so he packed his humps and set off across the desert, before the sun rose. He walked and he walked. The yellow sandy desert stretched out before him, as far as the eye could see.

The sun rose and the camel became very hot and thirsty, and he wanted to sit in the shade. All that he could see were some small cacti, but he was a tall camel and there wasn't enough shade for him. So he walked and walked some more, and still the desert stretched out as far as the horizon.

Changing the size

The pointer changes to a cross, and a dotted line shows you the size the picture will be.

1. To make a picture bigger or smaller, click on it once. A box and eight tiny squares appear around the picture. The picture is selected.

2. Move the pointer over one of the corner squares, so that the pointer changes to a double-ended arrow. Hold down the left mouse button.

3. The pointer is cross-shaped. Move the pointer toward the picture to make it smaller, and away to make it bigger. Release the mouse button and save.

'Wrapping' words around a picture

On this page, you can find out how to wrap words around a picture, like this, and how to move a picture if it's in the wrong place. You'll find that it's surprisingly easy – just follow the steps.

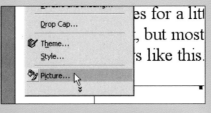

1. Move the pointer over the picture and click. Now click on Format, at the top of the screen, and on Picture. The Format Picture box appears.

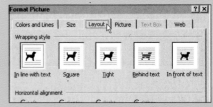

2. Click on Layout, at the top of the box. The white boxes below Wrapping style show you ways of arranging writing around a picture.

Square wrapping

3. To make writing flow around the picture in a square shape, as shown here, click on the box above Square. Click on OK, at the bottom of the box.

When you click, the picture stops being selected, and the insertion point appears.

4. To remove a blank line, position the pointer in the line, and click. The insertion point appears. Press the Delete key. The writing below moves up.

Tight wrapping

5. To make writing flow around a picture, click on the picture. Click on Format, and Picture, then on Layout. Click on the box above Tight, then on OK.

If you move the picture up and to the left, these words will move to join the words to the right of the picture.

6. If the writing is arranged strangely, you need to move the picture. Click on the picture once, then use the arrow keys to move the picture.

The writing is now arranged to the right of the picture.

7. When the writing is how you want it to be, move the pointer over another part of the page, and click. The insertion point reappears. Save and close.

Tips

1. To remove a picture, click on it, to select it. The box and tiny squares reappear. Press the Delete key on the keyboard.

2. You can also use the mouse to move a picture. Click on the picture, then hold down the mouse button. As you drag the mouse, the picture moves. A dotted line shows you where you have moved the picture. Release the mouse button.

27. A newsletter template

In Word, you can make a **template** that can be used as a base for any document that you create regularly. It's ideal for making newsletters, as whatever you put in a template appears every time you use it. You can even create a template that adds the date automatically. Follow the steps, but don't save until you're told to.

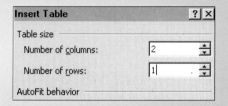

1. Click on the New document tool, and then on Table. Click on Insert, and on Table on the second menu. Type 2, press Tab, and type 1. Click on OK.

The pointer becomes a small black arrow. Click to select the writing.

2. The table is going to be the heading. Type the newsletter's name in the first cell. Move the pointer above the cell, and click to select the writing.

3. Change the style and size of the writing, to make it look more interesting. If you've forgotten how to do this, follow the steps on pages 24 and 25.

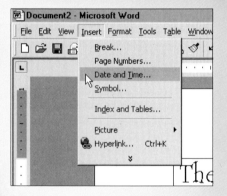

4. To add the date, press Tab, to move the insertion point into the second cell. Click on Insert, at the top of the screen, then on Date and Time.

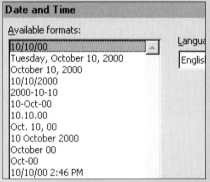

5. The Date and Time box appears. The date and the time are written in many ways. Click on one that you'd like to add to your newsletter.

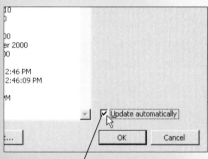

If there is already a mark in this box, you don't need to click on it.

6. To tell the computer to add the current date, each time you use the template, click on Update automatically, so that a check appears. Click on OK.

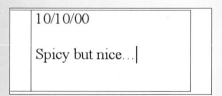

Be careful what you type – it will appear on every newsletter.

7. The date appears. Press Enter twice, then type some words. Press the down arrow key until the insertion point is below the table.

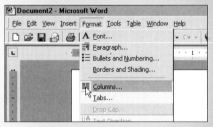

8. Press Enter twice, then click on Format, at the top of the screen. Click on the arrows at the bottom of the menu, and then click on Columns.

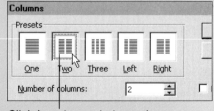

Click here to create two columns.

9. The Columns box appears. Click on Two, under Presets. A square appears, as shown above. This will create two columns for your newsletter.

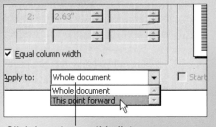

Click here to see this list.

10. Click on Whole document, next to Apply to, at the bottom of the box. A list appears. Move the pointer over This point forward, and click.

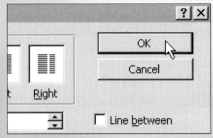

11. Click on OK, at the top of the Columns box. The box disappears. You can't see the columns on the screen, but they are there.

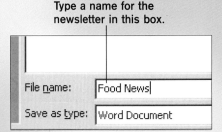

Type a name for the newsletter in this box.

12. Click on the Save tool, so that the Save As box appears on the screen. Type a name in the File name box, but <u>don't</u> click on Save.

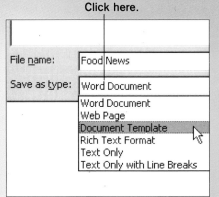

Click here.

The names on the list are different forms that you can save your work in.

13. In the white box next to Save as type, click on Word Document. On the list that drops down, click on Document Template.

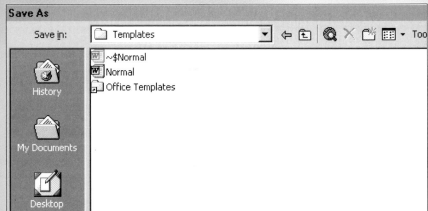

14. In the big white area are templates and folders that contain templates. When you have saved your template, it will join the others in this box.

15. Click on Save, then close the template by clicking on the cross in its top right-hand corner. Now find out how to use the template on page 54.

Don't forget! Everything in the heading will appear on every newsletter.

You can add different writing every time. Turn the page to find out how.

The date changes to the current date each time.

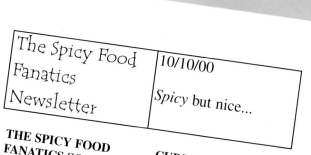

The Spicy Food Fanatics Newsletter

10/10/00

Spicy but nice...

THE SPICY FOOD FANATICS SOCIETY

Join the Spicy Food Fanatics Society TODAY, and you'll be in time to visit the amazing Jalapeno Jamboree, a spicy celebration of the jalapeno pe...

CURRY UP WITH THE QUIZ

We've already received hundreds of responses to the Curry Quiz, but the closing date is fast app...

ood 11/11/00

Spicy but nice...

er

JANT

success of last to places of food

FORTHCOMING SPICY FEATURES

Later this month, the So will be holding its third Annual Eat-Until-You- Competition. All mem are welco

28. Using a template

Once you've created and saved a template, you can use it again and again. You can type in it, change letter styles, and even add pictures. If you want to add a picture, you'll need to add it fairly early on, as adding a picture to a document that's full of writing can be tricky! Before starting, close any documents that are open.

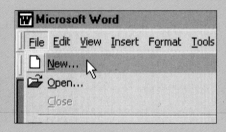

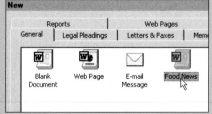

The Spicy Food Fanatics Newsletter | 10/10/00 | Spicy but

1. Creating a document from a template is slightly different than creating a normal document. Click on File, and then click on New.

2. The New box appears. Click on General, on the left-hand side, and you'll see your template. To open it, click on its name, and then on OK.

3. The template appears on the screen, with the insertion point in the top left-hand corner. The template automatically includes today's date.

Using a template

Words fill the left-hand column, then the right-hand column. When they reach the bottom of the page, they continue onto a new page.

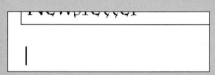

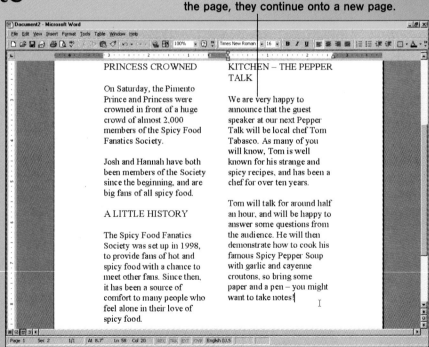

1. You need to make sure that the insertion point's in the right place. Press the down arrow key, until the insertion point will go no further down the page.

2. Start by typing a heading. As the words reach the middle of the page, they move onto a new line. This is because they're in an invisible column.

3. Press Enter twice, then type the first section. A long block of words forms down the page. Press Enter twice, then start typing the second section.

4. If you want to add a picture, use the mouse to move the pointer to where you want to add the picture, and click. The insertion point appears.

5. Press Enter three times, then follow the steps on pages 48-51, to add a picture. Save your newsletter as normal, but not as a template, and close it.

Deleting a template

If you create and save lots of different templates, it can be hard to find the one you want. Follow these steps to delete, or remove, a template. Close any documents that you've been working on, before you start.

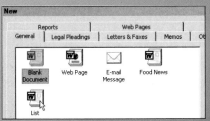

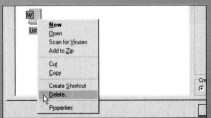

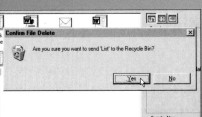

1. Click on File, and on New, as if you were opening a template (see page 54). In the New box, move the pointer over the template you want to delete.

2. Click the right mouse button. A menu appears. Move the pointer down the menu, so that it is over Delete. Now click the left mouse button.

3. A box appears, checking that you want to delete the template. Click on Yes, then click on the cross in the corner of the New box.

Templates can be used to create many things, such as score sheets or invoices. If you add a picture to a template, it will appear every time you use the template.

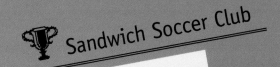

Sandwich Soccer Club

	Points
	3

The Spicy Food Fanatics Newsletter

12/12/00
Spicy but nice...

PIMENTO PRINCE AND PRINCESS CROWNED

On Saturday, the Pimento Prince and Princess were crowned in front of a huge crowd of almost 2,000 members of the Spicy Food Fanatics Society.

Josh and Hannah have both been members of the Society since the beginning, and are big fans of all spicy food.

A LITTLE HISTORY

The Spicy Food Fanatics Society was set up in 1998, to provide fans of hot and spicy food with a chance to meet... then, it has

HOT STUFF IN THE KITCHEN – THE PEPPER TALK

We are very happy to announce that the guest speaker at our next Pepper Talk will be local chef Tom Tabasco. As many of you will know, Tom is well known for his strange and spicy recipes, and has been a chef for over ten years.

Tom will talk for around half an hour, and will be happy to answer some questions from the audience. He will then demonstrate how to cook his famous Spicy Pepper Soup with garlic and cayenne croutons, so bring some paper and a pen - you might want to take notes!

Danny Digs
Gardening Specialist

Work done:

· All trees pruned and watered.
· All shrubs pruned and watered.
· Flowers planted throughout.
· Grass cut.
· Wooden fence built.
· General gardening advice.

Charge:

29. Finding a closed document

When you've saved and closed a document, it disappears from the screen. You need to know how you can find it again. If you share your computer with other people, finding your folder and the documents inside may be more tricky, but these steps show you how to find a document and open it, without too much trouble.

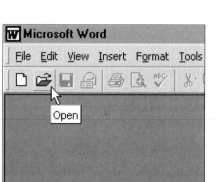

Your screen will look like this, when you've closed all documents.

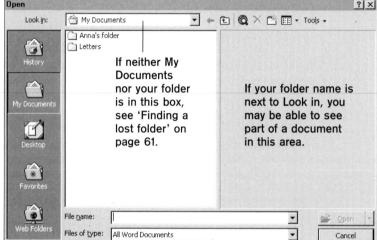

If neither My Documents nor your folder is in this box, see 'Finding a lost folder' on page 61.

If your folder name is next to Look in, you may be able to see part of a document in this area.

1. Before you start, close any documents that are open, then click on the Open tool, which is in the top left-hand corner of the screen.

2. The Open box appears. If My Documents is beside Look in, your folder will be in the box below. Click on the picture next to it, and go to steps 4 and 5.

3. If your folder name is next to Look in, you'll see the names of documents that you've saved, in the box below. Go to step 5, to open your document.

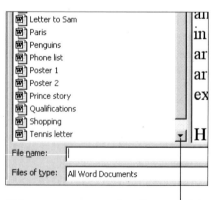

This arrow appears when there are lots of documents. Click on it to see more.

When you click, the document's name is selected.

4. Click on Open. The names of documents you've already saved are in the big white area. Find the name of the document that you want to open.

5. Click on the picture next to the document's name. Part of the document may appear in the Save As box. Now click on Open. The document appears.

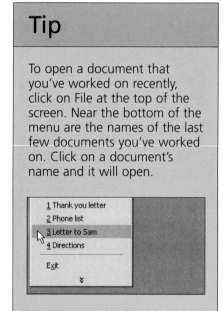

Tip

To open a document that you've worked on recently, click on File at the top of the screen. Near the bottom of the menu are the names of the last few documents you've worked on. Click on a document's name and it will open.

30. Switching off

It's important to switch off your computer the right way, or you may find that it doesn't work very well when you switch it back on. The best way to avoid problems is to follow the steps on this page.

Closing Microsoft® Word 2000

Before you close Microsoft® Word 2000, you need to save any documents that you've been working on. See pages 14-15, if you can't remember how to do this.

Click on the lower of the two crosses to close the document.

Click here to save the changes you've made.

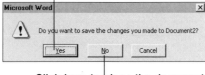

Click here to close the document without saving the changes.

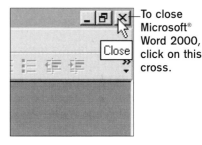

To close Microsoft® Word 2000, click on this cross.

1. In the top right-hand corner of the screen, you should see two crosses. Move the pointer over the lower cross and click, to close the document.

2. If this message appears, you've made changes since you last saved. To save, click on Yes, and turn to pages 14-15. Otherwise, click on No.

3. Close all open documents, then click on the cross in the top right-hand corner of the screen. Word vanishes and the Windows® screen reappears.

Shutting down

In computer jargon, switching off a computer is known as **shutting down**. Follow the steps below to shut down your computer.

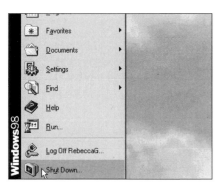

Click on Shut down so that a dot appears in the circle next to it.

Power buttons

1. Click on Start, as you did on page 6. The menu reappears. Move the pointer up, so that a dark bar is over Shut Down, then click the mouse button.

2. The menu disappears, and a box like this one appears. Click on Shut down, and then on OK. Wait while the computer gets itself ready to shut down.

3. The computer may switch itself off automatically. If not, wait until it tells you that it's ready. Press the on/off buttons on the system unit and monitor.

Handy tips

On this page, you can find out how to move several sections of writing around at once. You'll also find easy ways to select words, and a way to get help from your computer.

More about copying

In Microsoft® Word 2000, there's a feature that allows you to 'collect' several cut or copied sections. You can then choose which one to paste first.

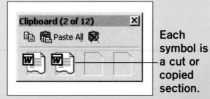

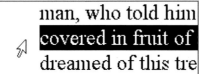

Each symbol is a cut or copied section.

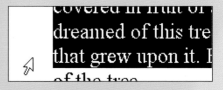

This is the first part of the section.

1. First use the mouse to select a section of writing. Now cut or copy it as you did on page 35. Then select a second section, and cut or copy it too.

2. The Clipboard appears, with symbols of pages on it. Position the insertion point where you want the section to appear in your document.

3. Rest the pointer over each page symbol, until you find the section you want. Click on the symbol. The section appears next to the insertion point.

Other ways to select

Each time the arrow key is pressed, a letter is selected.

To select a letter or a group of letters, move the insertion point to where you want to start selecting, and hold down Shift. Press the right arrow key.

To select one line of writing, move the pointer into the white area to the left of the writing, and click the left mouse button. The line is selected.

To select more than one line, move the pointer into the white area. Press and hold down the left mouse button, and move the pointer down the page.

Getting help

Word has a Help system, which you can get to by asking the animated Office Assistant questions. The Help system can be useful but also hard to understand. If you want to make the Office Assistant disappear at any time, move the pointer over it, and click the <u>right</u> mouse button. On the menu, click on Hide.

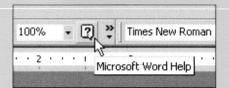

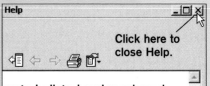

Click here to close Help.

1. To make the Office Assistant appear, click on the Help tool. The Assistant appears, and offers help. Type a word or a question, then click on Search.

2. The Assistant offers several options, so click on one to find out more. When you've found out what you need, close Help by clicking on the cross.

Computer words

the four **arrow keys** grouped together on the keyboard move the insertion point around the screen.

a **bullet** is a shape that you can add to pinpoint each item on a list.

a **CD-ROM** is a kind of disc that can transfer programs onto a computer.

a **cell** is a single box in a table.

clicking is pressing down and quickly releasing one of the buttons on the mouse, usually the left button.

you **close** a document when you have finished working on it and have saved it in a folder.

a **column** of cells is a vertical line of cells in a table.

when you **copy** something, it is remembered by the computer until something else is copied or cut.

when you **cut** something, it disappears and the computer remembers it until something else is copied or cut.

when you **delete** something, you remove it.

a **document** is Word's version of a page, or pages.

double-clicking is pressing down and releasing the left mouse button twice, very quickly.

dragging is moving the mouse, when the left mouse button is held down.

e-mail is sending messages on the Internet.

a **file** is another name for a document. Files are saved in folders.

a **folder** is where you store documents.

a **font** is a style of lettering.

the **hard disk drive** stores documents and stores programs and software that make a computer work.

hardware is computer equipment, such as the monitor.

a **header** is a heading that appears above the main area of a page, and is used for reference on every page.

in an **indented** line, the first word is positioned a small distance in from the left-hand edge of the line.

the **insertion point** is a small flashing line, which shows you where your typing will appear.

when you **install** software, you load it onto a computer, by transferring information onto the hard disk drive. Once this is done, the information stays there for you to use. You usually install software from a CD-ROM.

the **Internet** is a system that can link computers around the world.

when you **justify** writing, each line is the same length.

a **menu** offers you a list of options to choose from.

when you **paste** something that has been cut or copied, it appears next to the insertion point.

a **PC** (personal computer) is a computer that is usually used in homes and offices.

programs give a computer instructions. Microsoft® Word 2000 is a program, whereas Microsoft® Office 2000 is a group of programs that includes Microsoft® Word 2000.

a **row** of cells is a horizontal line of cells in a table.

saving is storing a document on a computer.

scrolling is seeing different parts of a document on the screen, by clicking on tiny scrolling arrows.

when you **select** words, a dark area appears over them. Selected pictures have eight tiny squares around them.

shutting down refers to the steps that a computer needs to take before you turn it off.

software is the name for computer programs. Software is usually stored on CD-ROMs.

the **system unit** contains the parts of the computer that process and store information.

a **template** is something that is used as a base for a document. It can contain words and pictures, and can be used again and again. It is ideal for creating newsletters or any other document that you produce regularly.

when you click on a **tool**, you tell the computer to do something. Tools are usually arranged on toolbars.

toolbars are lines of tools, grouped together.

undo reverses the last thing you did.

a **website** is a page or group of pages on the Internet.

wrapping is arranging words neatly around a picture.

Troubleshooting

Computers are complicated machines, and they can have problems. Hopefully you won't encounter many of them, but here are some helpful hints, in case something strange happens. If you get in a bind, remember it's actually pretty hard to 'break' a computer.

General troubleshooting tips

1. If you leave your computer for a while, you may find that the screen goes blank, or fills with colors or patterns. Just move the mouse, and the screen will return to how it was before.

2. If you can't see Start, try moving the pointer to the very bottom of the screen, so that it becomes a tiny black arrow. Hold down the left mouse button and drag the pointer upward.

3. If there's a page on the screen, but you can't see what you have been working on, try clicking on the scrolling arrows (see pages 16 and 47), to see if your work has moved off the screen.

4. If you think that you've lost a document, it may just be hiding behind another one. The name of each open document appears at the bottom of the screen in a rectangle. To see a document, click on its name.

5. If you accidentally double-click on a picture, the Format Picture box appears. To make it disappear, click on Cancel. Now click anywhere away from the picture, so that it is not selected.

6. Occasionally you may accidentally drag selected words across the screen, using the mouse. To move the words back to where they were, press Ctrl and Z or click on the Undo tool.

7. If the first letter on a line turns into a capital letter, you can change it into a little letter. Move the insertion point immediately to the right of the letter, press Backspace, and type the letter.

8. If your printer isn't printing, make sure it's switched on, and has plenty of paper and ink. If it still doesn't work, you'll need to look at the printer's instructions, or handbook.

9. If there's only one cross in the top right-hand corner of the screen when you're trying to close a document, more than one document is open. Clicking on the cross will close the first one.

10. To remove a row of cells from a table, move the insertion point into the row. Click on Table, at the top of the screen, then on Delete. Now click on Rows. The row disappears.

11. If a small menu suddenly appears on the page, you may have pressed the right mouse button. Move the pointer off the menu, and click the left mouse button. The menu disappears.

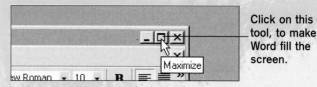

Click on this tool, to make Word fill the screen.

12. If you can see the Windows® screen around the edge of Microsoft® Word 2000, click on the Maximize tool, in the top right-hand corner of the screen. This will make Word fill the screen.

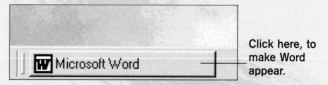

Click here, to make Word appear.

13. If you can't see the Microsoft® Word 2000 screen, it may have been hidden away. See if Microsoft Word appears in a rectangle at the bottom of the screen. If it does, click on it.

14. If you're adding a picture, and you see a box that tells you that the Clip Gallery cannot find it, click on Cancel, then click on the All Categories tool (see page 48). Now try another picture.

Looking for Microsoft® Word 2000

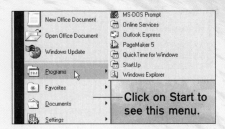

Click on Start to see this menu.

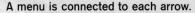
A menu is connected to each arrow.

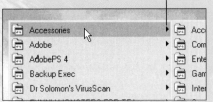

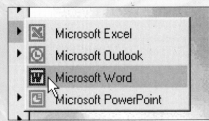

1. If you are trying to find out if you have Word installed on your computer, but can't find it on the second menu that appears, you may still have it.

2. Move the pointer over the first item on the menu that has a small arrow beside it. Click on it and another menu will appear. Look to see if Word is there.

3. If you see Word, click on it. If it's not there, click on each item on the menu with an arrow next to it. If you still can't find Word, you probably don't have it.

Finding a lost folder

If you're looking for a document, or trying to save something new, and you can't see your folder in the Open or Save As box, follow these steps to find it.

1. Look in the box next to Look in, or Save in, at the top of the Open or Save As box. If neither My Documents nor your folder name is there, see step 2.

2. To open My Documents, move the pointer over My Documents, on the left-hand side of the box. A line appears around it. Click once.

3. Your folder appears in the big white area. Click on it, then on Open. You'll see the names of documents that you've saved in the big white area.

Wizards

While you've been using Microsoft® Word 2000, you may have encountered the word 'wizard'. A wizard is a tool that asks a series of questions, and then creates a document such as a fax, resume or a memo, based on your answers. Once you've mastered the basics of word processing, by following the projects in this book, you should be able to start using wizards.

www.usborne.com

An e-mail address or **website** address that turns blue has become a hyperlink. This is a doorway into the **Internet**, which is a system that connects computers around the world. Press Backspace immediately, to change it back into normal writing. Don't click on it, as this may take you out of Word and into a different program. If you click on it by accident, and the screen changes, click on the cross in the top right-hand corner of the screen, to return to Microsoft® Word 2000.

Installing Microsoft® Word 2000

If Word isn't on your computer, you'll need to **install**, or load, it. When you buy it, either on its own or as part of Microsoft® Office 2000, you are given a disc, called a CD-ROM. On these pages, Word has been installed as part of Microsoft® Office 2000 Standard. If you have a different version of Office, or Word on its own, you may see slightly different things on your screen. You may also see different things if there has previously been a version of Office on your computer.

When you close all programs, the Windows® screen appears.

1. Before you start, close any programs you've been using. Find the CD-ROM drive on the system unit (see page 4), and press the button near the drive.

2. A drawer slides out. Place the CD-ROM in the drawer, with the writing facing up, and press the button again, to close the drawer. Wait for a moment.

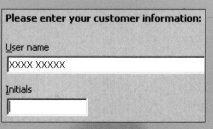

As you type, the words appear next to the insertion point. Press Backspace if you make a mistake.

3. The computer whirrs and a box appears in the middle of the screen. Wait for a while. The computer is getting ready to install the software.

4. After a while the appearance of the box changes. There are several white areas in the box. The top one has a flashing line in it. This is the insertion point.

5. Using the keyboard, type your name in the top white area. Now press the Tab key to move the insertion point into the second white area.

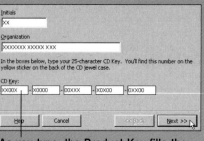

As you type, the Product Key fills the five white boxes. Make sure that you type it correctly.

Make a note of the Product ID number. You'll need it if you contact Microsoft® Technical Support.

6. Type your initials, then press Tab again. The insertion point is now below 'Organization'. Press the Tab key again, to move the insertion point below 'CD Key'.

7. Find the Product Key on the cover of your CD-ROM, and type it carefully. Now move the pointer arrow over Next, and click the left mouse button.

8. A new box appears. Find the number next to 'Product ID', write it down and keep it safe. Now look at the writing in the large white area.

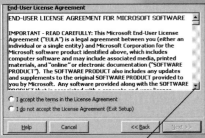

Click here to see the rest of the
End-User License Agreement.

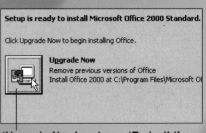

'Upgrade Now' replaces 'Typical' if an
earlier version of Microsoft® Word is on
your computer.

9. This is the End-User License Agreement, and it tells you things that you need to know about using the software. Make sure that you read it carefully.

10. Once you have read the Agreement, move the pointer over the circle next to 'I accept the terms...' and click. Now click on Next.

11. Another box appears. Click on 'Typical'. If you have an earlier version of Word on your computer, you'll see 'Upgrade Now' instead. Click on it.

12. A box appears and color slowly fills the white area. After a while, a second box tells you that the computer will restart. Just click on Yes.

13. The computer switches itself off and then back on again. A box appears on the screen. When color fills the white area, Word is installed.

14. Now take the CD-ROM out of the drawer, put it back in its cover, and keep it safe. To open Microsoft® Word 2000, follow the steps on pages 6-7.

After installing

Once you've installed Microsoft® Word 2000, you're ready to start using it, and ready to begin to use this book. However, first of all, you need to fill in your Registration Card, which is in the box that Microsoft® Office 2000 came in. When you've filled it in, send it to Microsoft, to let them know that you've installed Word on your computer. You'll find the address of Microsoft in your country in one of the leaflets in the software box.

Tip

As you're installing Microsoft® Word 2000, you may have to wait for a while, before each new screen appears. This is quite normal – the computer's got a lot to do. If you hear strange whirring noises, don't worry. Most computers make funny noises as they are installing software.

Index

Acknowledgements

Microsoft® Word 2000, Microsoft® Office 2000, Microsoft® Windows® 95 and Microsoft® Windows® 98 are either registered trademarks or trademarks of Microsoft Corporation in the United States and/or other countries. Screen shots reprinted by permission from Microsoft Corporation. Photos used with permission from Microsoft Corporation. This book is not a product of Microsoft Corporation.
Photographs of computers with permission from Gateway. Photographs of printers with permission from Hewlett-Packard Ltd.

Every effort has been made to trace the copyright holders of the material in this book. If any rights have been omitted, the publishers offer their sincere apologies and will rectify this in any future editions.